Your Free Gift (only available for a limited time)

Thanks for getting this book! If you want to learn more about various spirituality topics, then join Mari Silva's community and get a free guided meditation MP3 for awakening your third eye. This guided meditation mp3 is designed to open and strengthen ones third eye so you can experience a higher state of consciousness. Simply visit the link below the image to get started.

https://spiritualityspot.com/meditation

Contents

Introduction

Magic is used for different purposes in life. For instance, some use it in witchcraft, some use it to improve their lives, and others use it for luck and many other reasons. While there are various forms of magical powers, cord magic is present in the different things we use in our lives. A cord is one of the most commonly used magical tools. Cord magic is also known as knot magic since it involves tying knots during rituals and spells. This book focuses on cord magic and explains various aspects readers may want to know about this subject.

The primary purpose of this book is to enlighten people interested in learning all that cord magic has to offer. It acts as a practical guidebook for individuals who are passionate about practicing knot magic. Before learning about cord magic, it is imperative to understand the required tools and the entire practice. The essence of this guide is to teach you everything you need to become an excellent magician. Many people often associate magic with evil spells, but this is not the case with cord magic. You can dispel this myth by reading this excellent book.

This guide is unique in that it provides practical steps to follow when you perform cord magic. This information is not readily available since magic is associated with the supernatural world, meaning very few people have first-hand knowledge about what happens in the spiritual world. This guidebook is well-researched and provides you with all the details you need to learn about this esoteric subject. The internet is full of generic information about magic, but it may not add any value to your aspirations.

The guide is excellent for beginners since it is easy to understand and contains hands-on instructions that are easy to follow. The step-by-step approach to cord magic presented in this book is practical as it helps novices grasp the basic concepts involved quickly. The language used in this guide is simple and easy to follow. Apart from providing theoretical knowledge, you will also master practical skills that can help you perform various magical spells. With this copy, you may not need to consult professional magicians since you can get everything you want at your own pace.

If you are interested in learning cord magic, this is your ultimate guide in your journey. It teaches you all the different things you should know to create your knot magic spells and rituals. While there are different types of magic, this book gives you tips to empower your magic spells. The best thing you will realize in this workbook is that you can practice cord magic anywhere and anytime. Start now by hitting the "Buy Now" button and begin your cord magic journey!

Chapter 1: What Is Cord Magic?

Magic is available to witches through the most unexpected tools. A cord is one of the magical tools that witches often overlook. It is a simple tool, yet it is as powerful as any other source of magic that most people are familiar with.

Think about how you use cords in your everyday life. You might not view it from a magical perspective, but the fact is that there is magic in everything you do with it. When you tie your shoelaces, you do so thinking of your safety.

A considerable number of people tie cords into ribbons around their fingers; it is said that that ritual helps people remember things. What do you do when you have a crucial meeting at work? You put on a powerful tie to match the event. These reflect the subtlety of cord magic because it is neither complicated nor time-consuming.

Cords are probably the most flexible magic tool, and you can whip them into any shape you wish and return them to their natural forms to serve as poppits. One thing about cord magic is that it is present in many things that may not instantly come to mind.

Stringed musical instruments all have cords, meaning you can use them for magical purposes. Bards employed such instruments in performances filled with magical energy in the past.

Your vocal cords are also a form of a magical channel through which you can perform word magic. Hair braiding is another common source of cord magic. The word "tress" means "threefold" in French, and for hundreds or thousands of years, hair has been a restorative magic material.

For instance, witches used to place a lock of hair inside a decorative pendant to secure or protect the person the pendant was gifted.

Cord magic is also widely referred to as knot magic because it involves the tying or braiding of knots during spells and rituals.

The history of cord magic is vast and interesting. Historically, knots have always served a variety of ordinary and magical uses. In 400 B.C., historians used knots to memorize certain chronicles. People used them to count time for travel, count days between festivals, and observe various lunar rituals. The Hebrews even used knots in their alphabet and writing system.

In 1959, Gerald Gardner wrote about a *Cingulim*, a witch's cord usually around nine inches long or determined by the measurements of the witch's body.

The Cingulim symbolizes the witch's rank in witchcraft communities and traditions, and it is equally as crucial as a wand in many magical traditions. Some writings suggest that a teacher may ritually destroy it after a witch exits the coven or life. The teacher may also decide to hold on to it, depending on the traditions of that particular coven.

While at sea, sailors traditionally used knot magic to affect the weather around them; some untied knots to stir up the wind, and vice versa, depending on their needs at any specific time. Usually, they used three kinds of knots. Untied knots are used to bring about a gentle wind. The second type brought about a stronger wind while the third could herald a full-blown hurricane. Many communities still today use these spells.

Walking up to a high point wherever you are located and chanting your spell as you tie the first knot is one of such spell-casting rituals out there. Blow on the tied knot once and repeat for each knot according to their numbers, meaning you should blow twice for the second and thrice for the third.

Alexander the Great managed to release king-making powers held within a knot by the descendants of Gordias; he did so by untying an inextricable knot – or rather, slicing it in half!

The square knot, also known as the Knot of Heracles, is said to help wounds heal faster as it contains unmatched healing powers.

Even in old fairy tales for children, knots were frequently brought up; in a tale titled The Drummer, the protagonist goes about his adventures, untying knots, one at a time, from a knotted cord, to aid him throughout.

The ancient Druids used to hand-knot cords of various colors around their waist. These served as the identification of their craft specialty. The number of knots also indicated their ranks in the community.

Additionally, there is one called the Knot of Isis, with a looped and open design, resembling Ankh with its "arms" pointing below and representing the uterus. It is often paired with an amulet and sewn into priests' garments. It is also believed that the knot of Isis was often sewn into the wrappings of the dead.

A manuscript titled the *"Paenitentiale Theodori,"* or "Penitential of Theodore," tells the story of Theodore, a 7th-century Archbishop of Canterbury. The penitential was also a compilation of his offenses against God and the Church.

In the penitential, priests could find descriptions of specific sins and wrongdoings, with the steps that need to be taken by the sinner to expunge their sin from their record. An entry in the penitential forbids both priests and "laypeople" from taking credit for any "phylacteries," which are said to affect the soul. Such phylacteries imply an amulet, infused with a spell or sacred text, placed in a small bag that is then tied around the neck.

Magical prayers and symbols were often hidden from plain sight by Pagan practitioners; necklaces were then tied up with knots as they considered one of the most prominent places to place or hide a charm.

The power of cord magic lies in the symbolic value of the knots. Several spell books show that a knot can be used to bind a disease or spirit, and when loosened, used to stir up certain weather.

Outside of magical communities, people of different faiths use cords in meditation and prayer. The Catholics often use it for counting – the intensity of prayer or meditation heightens as you work upward along with a prayer bead or cord. The cord's color is also of significance to its ultimate purpose.

In Buddhism, there are special cords for different purposes. Cords can be blessed by a lama (teacher) through a mantra reading or a puff of air. In addition, before the invention of synthetic fabrics, many Buddhists wore their cords around their necks until they would organically disintegrate and fall off on their own. Some cords were also worn or used on special occasions only; some use them for vow-taking, and others use them as gifts to be given to a teacher for commemorative purposes.

Uses of Cord Magic

The simplest way to explain cord magic is that you tie knots in different materials. The idea behind this is that a knot represents life situations and individuals you're practicing magic with (or on). Knot spells vary from simple joining spells to binding spells to knots that last a lifetime.

Cord magic generally requires you to prepare your spells ahead of time and then use them accordingly. Over nine consecutive days, you can untie each knot to release the entrapped power. Typically, you need a piece of string to perform knot spells.

A witch may use yarn, thread, ribbon, twine, or any other knot-able material she has at hand. You can also use a piece of string. Some witches keep a dedicated stash of strings for spells, but you can use any material you find lying around.

It is a general rule of thumb to cleanse the material or fabric before use; this is done to eliminate any energies that may interfere with the spell. The process of doing this is called consecration, and you will learn more about it subsequently. A cord is a magical tool, unique to the witch who makes it; some even prefer using specific bundles of string or braids. Therefore, you are the only one who should ever use your cord.

There are many uses of cord magic, and perhaps the most common is the use of a knot as a container for power. In other words, you can store your magic in cords. The key is to visualize your desire being fulfilled as you tie your knot and chant the appropriate incantation.

As the power builds up, you continue to tie more knots until you reach the number nine. More will be discussed on this in a subsequent chapter.

Apart from this, there are several other uses of knot magic. Some are explained below.

Cords may be joined using directed energy, consecrated, blessed, and used as charms and amulets. Plus, you can collect cords and ribbons of diverse colors to represent something of great value.

One of the ways to use knot magic is in protection spells. A protection spell is done to magically keep you, your loved ones, or any other person safe from negative energies or psychic attacks. While braiding your cords together, you magically infuse the psychic energies you need into the knot.

You can then take your knotted amulet with you wherever you need protection. It can also be left or hidden in specific locations, such as the entrance of your home, to cast space-specific protection as well.

Below is a list of other ways to apply knot magic.

Cooperation

A witch may braid a specific number of cords together to symbolize something in particular. All cords used in the spell should be equal lengths to represent cooperation. You can then name each cord after certain individuals or situations with which you wish to foster cooperation. This spell is beneficial when a sense of disruption permeates the air in the presence of a certain group of people. In such cases, cord magic helps people harmonize their energies and ideas, just as knots do in certain spells. Focus the energy on the part of the braid where you need it the most.

Binding

A witch would wrap a cord around whichever objects she needed to bind for this act. In some cases, a puppet representing a troublesome person is used in such knot rituals to halt their negative energy and clear their intentions.

Deity Symbols

Gods and Goddesses can be represented by braided, knotted, bundled, balled, or colored cords placed in sacred spaces. You may braid a knot to symbolize divinity on your altar. Sometimes, a cord is placed around its witch's circle, representing the protective presence of a deity or mystical being from their faith. Some also create pieces from colored cords to be hung on their altars.

Joining and Releasing

Being one of the main aspects of knot magic, joining and releasing is said to be at its center. For instance, let's say you're on the lookout for a partner; use one cord to represent yourself and another for your crush. Proceed to tightly tie both cords together. Assuming you eventually find your person and establish a relationship, you will soon realize that they aren't who you initially thought they were. In such an unfortunate case, you simply disconnect the cords and go your separate ways.

Love and Relationships

Cord magic is generally used in matters of love and relationships, especially marriage. Most marriage vows usually include a declaration about ties binding both partners together. Joining two people together with specially prepared ribbons or cords is a tradition in pagan culture. The cords are then stored away with other meaningful items used in the ritual.

Such rituals can also be used on friendships or any relationships for that matter; a basic macramé half-hitch can be used to protect and secure a friendship. Specific colors and patterns that you feel represent your feelings for each other can be used. Then, exchange the bracelets on a significant date (such as the day you became friends) simultaneously.

Luck and Good Fortune

There are several methods of making enchanted luck or good fortune cords. One way is to use colored beads that represent your desire. For instance, let's say you want to make a knot spell for money. A sturdy piece of fabric or string would work well for that purpose; you can then tie some colored beads into it as you chant your incantation for each knot you tie. Green knots and beads are usually used for such spells.

Suppose you're doing a spell to improve your fortune in love and relationship; in such a case, pink knots and beads are usually used. Wear or carry around your knotted beads regularly to activate your ritual and bring more positive energy into your life.

Amulets

Amulets are a protective tool that can be created through various types of magic. You can create an amulet by tying a series of knots to protect your well-being, fight off sickness and diseases, or promote safety.

https://unsplash.com/photos/brown-leather-bag-on-gray-concrete-floor-4dvt0gsRU6A

Personal Development

Knot magic can be used to improve any aspect of your life. While focusing your intention on whichever aspect of your life you wish to improve, carry or wrap a colored, decorative cord around your hand. Whenever a relevant situation arises, reinforce your intent as you touch your cord.

To strengthen your spell, include a verbal spell that would activate your cord's energy whenever you touch it. Remember that you don't need a fancy word – a simple "On" can make the needed difference.

Weather Magic

As previously noted, sailors used knot magic to control and regulate the weather. For centuries, rope has had a central role in conducting weather magic and can also be incorporated into your cord magic witchcraft rituals.

A cord wrapped with knots representing the different states of the weather is necessary for this step. Sailors, for instance, always use a specific sailor's cord that represents three types of wind experienced. Context matters whenever you're setting your intentions; if you were a simple farmer, you could create a cord with each knot representing a different level of rain – showers, downpours, and or gentle rain.

There is a plethora of materials that can make for beautiful alternative cords, some of them being;

- Chains
- Laces
- Scarves
- Floss
- Sinew
- Leather
- Vines
- Wires
- Ribbons
- Ties

- Twine

- Threads

You can easily pick up all of these materials and much more from your local clothing store or craft shop, your kitchen, or even your local garden. In the next chapter, you will learn to choose the suitable fabric material for your knot spells.

Knot magic has since advanced from what it was then. Modern witches have increased accessibility to the materials listed above and other items used in knot spells and rituals. It makes cord magic accessible to everyone, including people new to the witchcraft community.

The knot, as noted earlier, serves as a conduit for energy. When you untie a knot, you release the magic, and when tied, a knot can serve protective purposes. It can be used to contain both the magic in its surroundings and within it.

Your knot's residual energy is more likely to benefit you as its owner. When untied, your knot's energy will be released into the universe, maybe lost forever. Since one can easily untie a knot, you can prepare specific "on" and "off" switches for your knot spells. However, be careful not to forget to set clear intentions for this as you create your spell.

The most traditional and commonly known cords have always been tied to knot magic (no pun intended!) Cords are pretty easy to tie and bind. Interestingly enough, the verb "tie" can imply *fastening, restricting, forming, and connecting* – all of these actions can be exercised in your knot magic spell craft.

Humans have consistently recognized and acknowledged this subtle connection, whether consciously or unconsciously – Muslims tie knots in their clothing as part of their pilgrimage rituals.

Celtics were also intimately familiar with knots, representing eternity to them, and Romans also used it for oaths. It is also quite intriguing to think that the word "magician" stands for "knot tier" in

Hebrew and Russian. In the Middle Ages, it was common for witches to hang knots over their home's doors to cast protection against any unwanted encounters with or influences from the mystical realm. Drawing a single continual line with your knots is known to be particularly effective.

These all show that humans (and witches) have always understood the subtle power of cord magic. It is one of the simplest forms of magic and one of the best places to begin if you're new to the witchcraft community.

In the contexts addressed above, tying a knot entails you're infusing a specific idea or thing therein. Particular knots, ones used for binding spells, can be kept intact for as long as needed – sometimes forever.

Perhaps the best thing about cord magic is that you can use knitting, crocheting, embroidery, applique, quilting, tatting, weaving, and other artistic techniques in the creation of your knot spells. They all give an advantage of creating something valuable when completed.

A simple advantage that knot magic has over some other forms of magic is that you can do it anywhere and at any time. It also doesn't require any obscure tools or materials.

One thing to always keep in mind is that knot magic is best practiced with natural substances. All-natural materials come from the earth, meaning they're already pre-charged with magical energy. Using a natural substance or material amplifies the magic in your knot spell.

Another thing to remember is never to use a cord more than once. Remember that each cord has its own intention. Mixing intentions can weaken and pollute your magic, rendering your spell ineffective or impotent.

In Wicca, knot magic is practiced in two ways: proactively and reactively. Taking a proactive approach to knot magic means preparing a spell ahead of time. For example, assuming that the hurricane season is due to start in two weeks, you go to supplies stores to get materials and items to board up your business or home. That is a proactive approach.

On the other hand, a reactive approach means rushing around a storm and trying to live through it.

Most knot magic spells are done proactively. You must always prepare in advance so you can magically improve a situation or avoid trouble.

Like all kinds of magic, the intent is fundamental in knot magic, and it is the only way to empower your spells successfully. As you read on, you will learn more about the position of intention in the creation of knot magic spells and rituals.

The next chapter delves into the process of choosing the perfect fabric for cord magic. You'll learn what kind of fabric to go for and why to go for it.

Chapter 2: Choosing Your Fabric

Everything is magical; this is a fact in witchcraft. There are hundreds of resources that highlight the magical properties of trees, colors, gemstones, and even fabrics, and these properties are essential guides in your magical journey. They help to narrow down your focus and amplify your magic with theirs.

The whole point of using specific materials for specific spells is strengthening the spell with the materials' magic. For example, suppose you wish to make a talisman for money. In that case, your spell is more likely to be effective if you use materials with magical properties related to wealth, luck, good fortune, etc.

The way a fabric is made, the material it is made from, its history and mythology, and its properties can all strengthen or weaken a magic spell. Therefore, you must try as much as possible not to limit yourself to only color when working with fabrics.

Since knot magic deals directly with the use of fabrics, you must have as much knowledge as possible about the different fabrics you will be working with.

In this chapter, we will discuss the *correspondences*, the various fabrics out there, and the meanings they each hold, as well as their magical properties. Correspondences are influenced by the fields of history, folklore, mythology, and dream symbols.

There are also many resources available online, from fun facts, trivia, and extended information to sources that flesh out each magical property. A well-planned research session can broaden your horizons with information about how such fabrics, rituals, myths, folklores, and histories were perceived and used by different communities in the past.

You can also find comprehensive lists of materials with descriptions of each fabric and how it is made. Knowing this information by heart will help you more organically know which fabrics to use for which specific rituals or purposes; you'll have a deeper understanding of how each fabric can affect your overall ritual in its own way.

There are many subtle differences and inconsistencies that might fly over your head if you're not well-read enough about the matter; flannel, for example, is often made from wool, synthetic fibers, and cotton. However, wool flannel may give an entirely different effect compared to that of cotton flannel. The same applies to other similarly and variously customized fabrics; a piece of linen made from flax will naturally differ from one made from hemp.

This chapter aims to help you unravel the magic of fabrics and how to use them to your advantage. Anyone who's been part of the witchcraft community knows that every item, material, and symbol used in a spell or ritual adds to the magic.

Fabrics have different types of energies. Some are capable of offering mystic protection against negative energies. Therefore, this knowledge can be quite helpful in the practice of knot magic. It can also be extremely practical for other or supplementary uses as well: making ritual robes, talismans, pouches, magical cords, or any other object that you may need or want for your witchcraft practices. The possibilities are limitless.

Canvas

- **Correspondences:** New beginnings, creativity, possibilities, and potential

- **Astrological Sign:** Virgo

Marquees, tents, backpacks, sails, shelters, and even support structures for oil paintings are all made from canvas. The fabric is also widely popular in the fashion industry since it is used to make shoes, handbags, and technological device cases because of its highly durable nature. A canvas is plain-woven and highly versatile.

Cashmere

- **Correspondences:** Luxury, comfort, warmth

- **Astrological Sign:** Capricorn

You have probably heard about cashmere and might even have one or two cashmere sweaters. But are you familiar with its origin and magical properties? Cashmere is considered one of the best fabrics in the magical world and a multi-faceted fiber globally.

Cashmere is a natural fabric, and it comes from an animal – similarly to wool, silk, and other hairs or furs. It is in the same category as merino wool, sheep's wool, mohair, and other common natural fibers that you might have heard of.

It is a naturally occurring fiber. Therefore, it is more valuable in a spell or ritual than any artificial synthetic because it has natural properties and offers many benefits, spiritual and otherwise.

Cashmere comes from goats, which are considered "clean" animals in the Jewish belief system. In the history of some traditions, it is custom to honor special or esteemed guests by sacrificing goats. According to folklore, Napoleon bought his second wife seventeen cashmere scarves, and she loved them so much that cashmere became instantly popular among the aristocrats.

As you can tell from its correspondences, cashmere is best used in knot spells relating to comfort, warmth, and luxury. For example, you can use this fabric in a spell for sleep improvement.

Cotton

- **Correspondences:** Protection, good luck, harvest, simplicity, rain.

- **Astrological Sign:** Virgo

- **Element:** Earth

Cotton has been used as a clothing material since ancient times. It comes from the cotton plant, which means it is a natural fabric. It is commonly used for various clothes and garments, from blouses to pants, bed linen, and even underwear.

Since cotton comes from a natural plant source, it has powerful magic properties. It is believed that clothes made from cotton and other natural fibers can attract the Divine into an environment. Compared to non-synthetic fabrics, cotton can retain greater magical energies. It can also offer protection from negative energies and entities.

It was believed that if one wanted some rain, they could burn some cotton to make that happen. Some also scattered it in their surrounding environment to cast and keep out ghosts or negative spirits. In Georgian black culture in the United States, it is believed that a newlywed couple who spend their wedding night on a cotton mattress will always be blessed with financial security.

You can use cotton in spell work relating to good fortune, luck, protection, and money.

Chiffon

- **Correspondences:** Vulnerability, elegance, femininity, delicacy.

- **Astrological Sign:** Gemini

- **Element:** Air

Chiffon is commonly used for evening wear, lingerie, bridal, and accessories due to its breathability. However, the best thing about this fiber is that it has common fabric contents such as silk and cotton.

https://unsplash.com/photos/teal-and-black-ribbon-on-white-surface-FRioMqel66A

In other words, chiffon has similar magical properties to silk and cotton. Therefore, you can use it for any spell you would use a cotton or silk fabric for. Today, most chiffon materials are made of polyester, which is an artificial fiber.

So, you're better off using silk chiffon in your knot spells since it is a natural fiber. You may use chiffon to make knots for the Divine feminine or other feminine deities. There are different kinds of chiffon, so be careful when purchasing it for a spell or ritual.

Flannel

- **Correspondences:** Comfort, warmth, relaxation, mojo bags.

- **Astrological Sign:** Cancer

- **Element:** Earth

You may be surprised to learn that the best flannel quality that anyone could initially get their hands on was the Turkish red flannel. In fact, a considerable number of mojo bags are made of red flannel.

kelly, CC BY-SA 2.0 https://creativecommons.org/licenses/by-sa/2.0 via Wikimedia Commons https://commons.wikimedia.org/wiki/File:Overlap_of_flannel_fabric.jpg

This tradition goes back to the period of the slave trade, or even before then. Since flannel was quite affordable and relatively durable, slaves used it to make underwear. They even thought that Flannel underwear helped prevent dysentery and diarrhea during the 1880s. The flannel scraps that remained from making the underwear were also used by slaves to make mojo bags.

As we mentioned above, flannel can be made of several materials. They mainly used wool during ancient times. There is also cotton flannel and flannel made of synthetic fabrics. This is something that you need to be very attentive to when using flannel for your knot spells. Each type of fabric is associated with a different symbol and attracts different things, which is why using the wrong type of flannel can affect the quality of your spell. Check the fabric's label, search the manufacturer's website, or ask a trusted retailer about the fabric's contents before using it in your knot spell.

Flax

- **Correspondences:** Prosperity, man weakness, Queen Hulda, God-given gifts

- **Astrological Sign:** Gemini

Flax is seeds derived from a flax plant and is of incredible significance in the witchcraft world. Flax fabric can help you manifest great things and retrieve amazing results if used wisely.

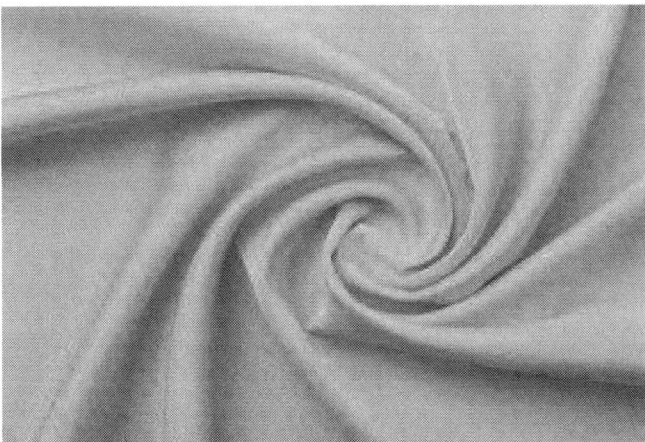

https://pixabay.com/zh/photos/fabric-curtain-brown-texture-5259683/

Ancient Egyptians valued Flaxseeds greatly as they were considered a God-given blessing. You can spot a plethora of woven linen and fabrics made from flax scattered around ancient Egyptian temples and tombs. On top of that, watching over the cultivation and spinning of flax seeds was Hulda, a Teutonic goddess who was mentioned in many ancient writings. Some believe that Hulda also taught others how to spin flax and make fabric out of it.

In Estonian culture and history, the "Flax Mother" was thought to reside in a linen press, guarding the flaxseeds. The references mentioned above, and much more, are a testament to how valued flax is in many cultures and traditions.

Hemp

- **Correspondences:** Burial, travel, doors, and open gates, trance, enlightenment, Bastet, and vision.

- **Astrological Sign:** Capricorn

- **Element:** Spirit

https://pixabay.com/zh/photos/ball-cord-hemp-natural-twine-88303/

Hemp fibers were used to make sails for the boats, as it was the only material strong enough to hold up against the aggressive nature of the ocean winds. Those who passed away were also buried in hemp, perhaps because hemp was believed to be a sacred plant derivative to the Bastet, the Egyptian goddess associated with pleasure, protection, and the attractor of good well-being and health. Ancient Egyptians would burn sacred incense containing cinnamon and cannabis flowers to honor Isis, or the goddess Bastet. In another part of the world, hemp plants, or Paji ma, were worn by Korean men for the belief that they enhanced masculinity and attracted power.

Gauze

- **Correspondences:** Healing and wealth ambiguity
- **Astrological Sign:** Gemini
- **Element:** Air

According to dream symbolism, those who dress up in gauze tend to have feelings of ambiguity or uncertainty regarding their wealth. This is typical because gauze was made strictly out of silk long ago.

Turning this luxurious fabric into gauze meant that manufacturers had to pierce holes through the fabric, which makes sense as to why gauze was associated with uncertainty regarding a person's welfare.

Today, several materials can be used to make gauze. However, you don't see people parading around in outfits made of this fabric. Cotton gauze is often used to wrap wounds and serve other medical purposes in a medical context.

Lace

- **Correspondences:** Rite of passage, sexuality, femininity, sensuality, sacredness, duality, and privilege.
- **Element:** Lace

Around 1500 years ago in Europe, the earliest forms of lace emerged. People tied linen threads and fabrics to each other to make this intricate fabric. While the exact origin of this fabric is unknown, many experts argue that it was either Belgium or Italy. Lace is most eminent in wedding dresses, especially among members of the

European nobility. There are generally four types of lace: Duchess Lace, Renaissance Lace, Rosepoint Lace, and Princess Lace. However, two of them - Duchess Lace and Rosepoint Lace - are considered antique lacing techniques and are no longer practiced today.

Lamé

- **Correspondences:** Wealth, royalty, sun, moon, and luxury

- **Astrological Sign:** Leo

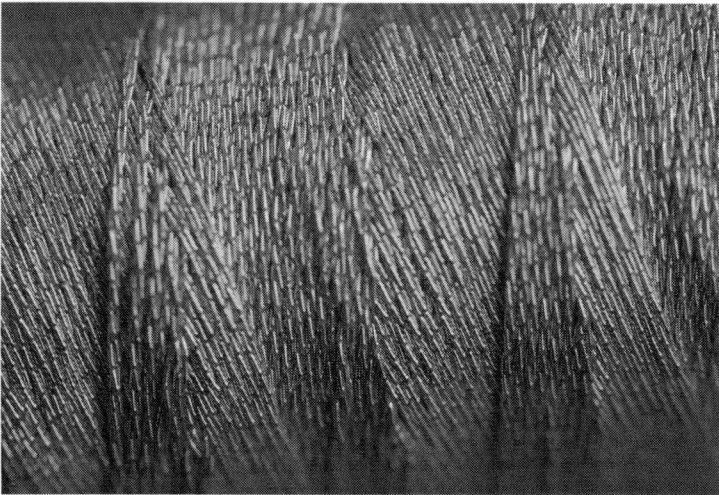

https://pixabay.com/zh/photos/thread-yarn-gold-thread-coil-1163914/

During ancient times, gold and silver yarn was used to make clothing pieces from start to finish. Before the creation of lamé, silver and gold were delicately wrapped around cotton or silk yarn to create clothing articles that would suit the grandeur of princesses. This was until lamé, a luxurious fabric, came to life. Silver, gold, and copper, at times, are used to make Lamé. Instead of being wrapped around cotton or silk, these metals are woven or knitted with other metallic fibers, like stainless steel or aluminum threads.

Leather

- **Correspondences:** Animals, protection, covering, and instinct

- **Astrological Sign:** Taurus

- **Element:** Earth

Leather has always been a very popular and versatile fabric and can be dated back to 3000 BC. The Romans used leather to make sails for their boats to ensure durability and sturdiness. They also used it to make weapons, furniture, and tents. Around 1000 years later, ancient Egyptian women started using leather and made a significant fashion statement by being the first to use them as articles of clothing. Interestingly, it was popularly used as a home wallpaper during the 17th century, especially in hotspots like Venice and Florence. If you think about it, each person wears around 4 leather items on average. This sounds like a lot at first glance. However, this includes belts, wallets, shoes, watch straps, purses, and other clothing and accessory items.

Linen

- **Correspondences:** Purity, elegance, righteousness, luxury, light, rest, and sophistication. Linen is widely favored because it absorbs sweat and moisture and releases it almost instantaneously.

- **Element:** Spirit

Interestingly, linen was used as a currency by ancient Egyptians. They also used the fabric to wrap their mummies. Priests also said their prayers and wrote down on the fabric while wrapping the deceased in linen.

The Irish believe that linen can absorb energy, which is why cloth strips were thought to be appropriate offerings. In Ireland, prayers were infused into the cloth strips before being hung on trees.

Linen, as a fabric, is highly sacred. In fact, the bible has mentioned or referenced the fabric over 100 times. It symbolizes success and worldly power and is often worn by the most affluent, influential, and important individuals.

Fine linen is often referred to or mentioned whenever "righteous and pure" women were brought up in ancient cultures and beliefs.

Moreover, god-worshipping temples were often dressed in fine linen, and people who visited the temple were also expected to dress in the same fabric.

Satin

- **Correspondences:** Sensuality, lustrousness, love, and shininess.
- **Astrological Sign:** Libra
- **Element:** Fire and water

https://unsplash.com/photos/green-textile-Th_WZMUPnO4

Satin is used for making the more expensive and finer satins. Satin was the only available material for making silk during the Middle Ages, which explains why it was reserved for the more financially privileged individuals. However, other types of satin, which can be commonly found nowadays, are made of lower-grade or less luxurious fabrics, such as polyester and nylon, making it possible for common citizens to enjoy using the shiny fabric.

Silk

- **Correspondences:** Luxury, smoothness, wealth, transformation, softness, prestige, and magical insulation.

- **Astrological Sign:** Libra

- **Element:** Water

https://unsplash.com/photos/blue-textile-on-white-textile-n29rGnbTid4

Silk is among the most luxurious fabric in the world, and it also holds an incredible significance in the world of magic and witchcraft. According to magicians, silk serves as a "natural magical insulator," meaning that the fabric can keep all the magical properties buried deep within itself. It hides and protects the magical properties from the external world and its influences.

Velvet

- **Correspondences:** Honor, leadership, sensuality, distinction, royalty, and emotions.

- **Astrological Sign:** Leo

- **Element:** Fire

https://unsplash.com/photos/red-textile-in-close-up-photography-MuUwn0geeec

Velvet is often made of cotton, synthetic fibers, or silk. The word velvet comes from a middle French word, "velu," which means shaggy. This fabric was featured in countless paintings and was a symbol of royalty, status, and leadership. Velvet was also a main character in a lot of portraits made for figures of authority, such as queens, significant political figures, and leaders.

Voile

- **Correspondences:** Hidden, secrets, unveiling, and weddings.
- **Astrological Sign:** Gemini
- **Element:** Air

The word "voile" is also derived from French and means veil. The fabric is semi-sheer and very lightweight. Voile is 100% woven cotton fabric. It usually has a higher thread count, and its weave appears to be much tighter than other cotton fabrics, making it feel incredibly soft and silky. Voile is characterized by its very light drape and is often used to make wedding dresses and veils.

Wool

- **Correspondences:** Renewal, female crafts, hope, comfort, spinning, durability, and warmth.
- **Astrological Sign:** Aries
- **Element:** Earth

https://unsplash.com/photos/assorted-color-thread-lot-o-d37kiKqqc

According to the bible, wool is associated with everything free of sin. It is very clean and pure, which is why it should never be mixed with linen. If mixed, it would simply lose its purity. As God's children, we are often referred to as sheep, and Jesus Christ is also often depicted as the "Lamb of God."

Metals

Base Metals

1. **Aluminum:** It is considered as a magician's "invisibility metals." Aluminum can help us see energies that are yet to come our way. It serves as an incredible foundation for a magic mirror when worn as jewelry.

2. **Tin:** We often forget that metals are made of crystals, and tin is the perfect reminder of this phenomenon. It helps us see that metals are not always hard, and they look that way because of the environment in which they were placed. Tin is incredibly helpful and easy to work with, as this element is incredibly cooperative.

3. **Copper:** Everyone knows that copper is a primary conductor of heat and electricity. It also serves as a bridge between several physical and spiritual concepts, making it excellent for magic wands. If used correctly, specialists can use copper to get rid of negative energy.

4. **Iron:** Iron, as you know, is the core of the Earth. It is also the heart of the entire universe. Iron is spiritual and terrestrial, making it perfect for grounding techniques and other stellar work. Specialists often use iron to aid in completing out-of-body experiences, as it offers a link between our realm and others.

5. **Nickel:** This metal is out of this world - literally. It links to the majority of other dimensions in existence. It is a very complicated metal. When mixed with an alloy, the metal can

make the mix utterly complex, which is deemed helpful whenever we need to find answers, solve problems, obtain information, or make personal breakthroughs.

6. **Lead:** Lead is ideal for black space meditations as it vows to create silence, making it an excellent metal for blocking all types of energy. It can also be used to keep magic in or out.

Precious Metals

Gold: Gold is associated with anything related to wealth, growth, and health. It is a sun metal and is all about the gradual path toward accomplishment and success. However, you need to keep in mind that most gold you find today are alloys, and the only pure form of gold is 24k.

Silver: Silver, as you probably already know, is a high-level conductor of heat and electricity. You can think of silver as a flowing river that transports the various elements. The unique thing about silver is that it absorbs but never holds captive. It cannot store, yet its processing abilities make it a great metal for various magical charms and spells.

Many witches craft their tools, talismans, and pouches using materials that match the goals of the spell. They use fabric for their spells, choosing colors that align with their goal and intent. But one thing that many may not understand is that the fabrics themselves are just as crucial in the process.

Chapter 3: Color Matters

Color is a vital part of magic and witchcraft. It channels the energy in your mind, whether you realize it or not. This is evident in how different colors elicit different reactions in us. For instance, a child reacts differently to a brightly colored room than a more somber one. Your energy can shift depending on the colors in your environment.

https://unsplash.com/photos/red-yellow-and-blue-textile-20T7ctRArtA

Consciously or subconsciously, the predominant color in your immediate environment can dramatically influence your thoughts, feelings, moods, and vitality. Since color is unbelievably subtle, it is easy to overlook it as a source of magic. Fortunately, this subtlety is precisely why it provides witches with a wide array of potential magical applications – meaning you can apply colors in various forms of modern witchcraft.

You might have heard about witches harnessing the power of colors in magical activities. For example, let's say you have a striking red lipstick that you always wear on your first dates because you know how fiery it is.

It may not be immediately evident, but that is a form of color magic, with seduction being the ultimate goal. The ability to inspire specific feelings or reactions in another person through your lipstick color is a testament to the magic of colors.

Do you often find that you feel great comfort in lying on the grass on a warm day? If yes, that is you immersing yourself in the soothing properties of the sun's colors: yellow and gold.

Perhaps the most appealing thing about color magic is that you use it every day without even realizing it. It is woven into the very fabric of your life, just by influencing the choices you make daily. In other words, you're likely already practicing more magic than you realize.

Color magic invokes magical responses through the color spectrum and each color's properties, correspondences, and intention. Color matters more than most people think, and knot magic and color magic are intertwined.

Each color in a knot contains a field of energy, within which is an embedded energetic meaning. Each also corresponds to a magical meaning. In the witchcraft community, these are referred to as magic color correspondences.

Learning more about the energy and uses of different colors can help you more accurately supercharge your cord magic practices for certain situations. You are the only one who has to know how a specific cord color is helping you.

To conspire with the universe's magic, you can use color to enhance and amplify your inner magic significantly.

Combining cord magic plus color magic requires you to determine the type of spell you want to perform. Is it a consecration ritual, blessing ceremony, magic spell, charm, amulet, enchantment, or a combination of these? Then, you must choose the colors that best represent your will or intention.

It is also integral to note that each color also has its own astrological power and meaning. Being familiar with such information can be extremely influential in your work as you are then aware of how each color aligns with your zodiac and the type of energy you can extract from it.

As is commonly known, each of us is born under a specific astrological (or zodiac) sign. This system helps magic practitioners easily tie color sequences to their relevant astrological signs.

The term "zodiac" roughly entails an *animal belt* suspended between our Earth and heaven. This belt is said to be circular, divided into 12 categories, each of them encompassing 30 degrees. The different segments are then linked to specific constellations.

Each of the different cardinal elements (Earth, air, fire, and water) are correlated to a group of the zodiac signs, as well as a specific animal. In Chinese philosophy and culture, each element is associated with a specific variety of colors. Therefore, the astrological signs are naturally connected to different colors.

So, even if you have a favorite color or colors based on your preferences, specific color sets are associated with your zodiac sign. Working with these colors when you perform any magical exercise is the surest way to ensure the efficacy of your magic.

This chapter extensively discusses colors blends and how you can choose the ones best suited for you, depending on your intention and goal.

While most witches agree on the general properties of colors, always remember that you are the most critical part of any spell. You are your magic. Every witch relates to colors in unique ways. So, you shouldn't hold yourself back from experimenting with colors until you find the perfect blend for you.

Do not think of this chapter as a definitive guide that must be adhered to no matter what. Instead, consider it a general guide with suggestions that can be improved on as you advance in your magical practice.

Before delving into the colors, consider a few things about combining cord magic with color magic.

First, always pick the color of your cords according to the objective of your spell or ritual. Or you can use them as elemental markers. For example, yellow can represent the east, red for the south, green for the north, and blue for the west.

Your altar cloth should have the right colors for sacred reasons. Many witches often use white because it is pure. However, it is not always easy to keep clean. So, you might want to use another color.

Also, as you're creating talismans, charms, or amulets, try to use objects and cords in varying hues and tones. For example, you can use bright red strings for an "attracting love" charm.

For quick access, you can categorize your magical items, be they herbs, spices or blends, etc., by the colors that match up with their corresponding properties and intentions.

An integral aspect of forming your intention for a spell is proper visualization. When you visualize, envision various colors entering your body and spirit in the form of light. This is particularly effective for witches who combine chakra work with spell and ritual work.

Additionally, always wear clothes that reflect the energy you wish to attract in your daily life, and this also applies to accessories. Remember that color can cause subtle shifts in how you experience each day.

Have the relevant color correspondences in mind as you choose your spell's components. You can also adjust the ambiance of the space where you'll conduct your ritual by utilizing colored bulbs to your liking. If you don't have access to colored bulbs, you can opt for hanging sheer curtains or fabrics in specific colors so that some sun rays can shine through and disperse the energy you've intended for into your surroundings. Don't forget to use different colored paper while putting together different parts of your spell book.

A color's tone and hue matter just as much as the primary shade itself. The tone of a color determines its overall intensity. Bright and vibrant tones are typically used to channel radiant and active energy. Their vibrancy and crisp visual volume make your intentions clear to your own subconscious and the universe above.

Darker hues, however, are more suited for grounding and settling atmospheres, inspiring a restful and relaxing state of mind.

On the other hand, muddy tones of colors can weaken the effects of a magic spell or ritual unless you use them as a substitute for other items. For example, you can replace a mustard seed with mustard yellow if you can't find the former for a spell.

Here's a more comprehensive example:

Grass green is connected to growth. Emerald green is excellent for accenting prosperity. Lime green attunes you with your inner child.

Primary blue is connected to a feeling of joy. To get in touch with some inner serenity, a bright sky blue could work. On the other side of things, dark blue accents a more conventional or organized aura as it is on the more formal side.

As you can see, each shade of a single color is associated with different feelings. You must always consider this when doing knot spell work or any other form of magic in general.

However, the most crucial thing to never forget is that correspondences matter very little if you don't form a personal connection with colors. Your own connection with or perception of the color does not have to align with the conventional meanings associated with them.

Most people have a distinctive and personal emotional and mental connection to a color, altering what it symbolizes for them; you can apply such colors in all stages of your spell work. The meaningful personal connection is a sufficient foundation for the energy you need.

Below are some colors and their magical correspondences.

Red

- **Element:** Fire
- **Chakra:** Root
- **Astrological Sign:** Aries
- **Energy:** Masculine

The color red is the hue of fire and passion, symbolizing flame and rebirth. Representing protection, energy, power, love, fertility, sexual vitality, motivation, and life's essence, red is a widely appreciated color. It strongly vibrates with vibrance and is perfect for travel, adventure, and happiness. It is also commonly used to ignite passion towards a person or situation.

People born between March 21st and April 20th are under the sign Aries, and red is their representative color. Aries is an active fire sign, meaning that you have powerful positive energy and a drive for success. Closely linked to the planet Mars, the ram also symbolizes Aries.

The fiery strips of red reflect the strength and perseverance that everyone born under this sign carries. Historically, the color red has been strongly associated with love and violence, and both of these have a single defining factor: passion.

Red represents fervor and devotion, despite some people's perceptions that it is an extremely aggressive or violent color.

Physiologically, the color red has a noticeable impact on the body. It increases heart rate, blood pressure, and overall excitability in people. In other words, it works as a physical stimulant.

So, suppose you want to do a spell relating to love, lust, or passion. In that case, red is your go-to color. As an Aries, using red strings in knot spell works can boost the efficacy of your spell and increase the likelihood of success.

Pink

- **Element:** Earth
- **Chakra:** Root
- **Astrological Sign:** Taurus
- **Energy:** Feminine

Pink is a quieter version of the color red. It represents friendly, kind, and romantic feelings and inner peace. Some say it is a blend of the fire and air element, but the earth is its cardinal element. This color is often used in spells to conjure the magic of romance, but that's not all.

The color pink represents romantic love, affection, romance, emotional maturity, nurturing, caring, peace, morality, emotional healing, etc.

It is also used to bestow kindness, softness, feminine charms, femininity, and to heal emotions. In magic spells, hot pink can attract flirtatious energy - it vibrates with laws of attraction and chemistry. You're a Taurus if your birthday is between April 20th and May 20th, and your primary color is pink. Taurus is associated with Venus, so it is also linked to the goddess Aphrodite or Venus. As you may already know, Aphrodite is the goddess of love, so it makes sense that this color is strongly linked to romantic feelings.

Imagine you want to bless a newborn girl. In that instance, baby pink would be an appropriate option. You may use pink cords in spells related to friendship, harmony, diplomatic interaction, etc.

Silver (White)

- **Element**: Water
- **Chakra:** Crown
- **Astrological Sign:** Cancer
- **Energy:** Feminine

White is a spiritual color. It represents the Divine or the greatest good. It represents consciousness, wisdom, spiritual connection, and the highest forms of good. It also symbolizes sensitivity, grace, and mysticism. The magic of white makes it perfect for consecration and purification spells.

You can use it to summon divine light, angels, blessings, and spirituality. You can also utilize white to summon remedial energies to help you correct mistakes. White's astrological sign is cancer. If your birthdate is between June 21st and July 22nd, your sign is cancer, and your color is silver/white.

Silver/white is strongly associated with success and wealth. However, it also has a seemingly dangerous side. In ancient cultures, it was considered a symbol of deceit, insincerity, and enigma. Opting for too much silver might make you seem deceitful or evasive, so try to keep it to a minimum in your everyday wardrobe.

Furthermore, this color and its hues are connected with moon gods. It can be used in spells that reflect a search for meaning, a call to a higher purpose, or an intrinsic urge to rise beyond your current circumstances.

You might consider including some minimal silver cords or chains into your life as a fashion statement, which is known to increase inner strength without overwhelming you.

Gold (Yellow)

- **Element:** Fire

- **Chakra:** Solar Plexus

- **Astrological Sign:** Leo

- **Energy:** Masculine

The colors gold and yellow are often used interchangeably in magical practices. They both symbolize leadership, blessing, health, and productivity. Yellow can either be pale or vibrant. Pale yellow corresponds to the air element, while vibrant yellow corresponds to the fire element. But ultimately, gold and yellow are both considered fire colors.

Gold is often used in matters of communication, charisma, and creativity. It depicts the things you yearn for and hope for. It is the color of intelligence, personal success, experience, and self-awareness, according to witches. It carries the energies of abundance, glamour, wisdom, and leadership.

The astrological sign of gold is Leo and ruled by the planet sun. If you were born between July 23rd and August 22nd, your sign is Leo. Therefore, using these colors in your magical workings can boost the efficacy of your inner magic.

You can feel that gold represents glamour and elegance as soon as you see it. The material originates from the earth and has long been used as a symbol of power, status, and strength in many civilizations. Gold was associated with divinity in several medieval Christian civilizations.

Use the color gold in spells for safe travel and adventure. To instill mental clarity in yourself or another person, utilize lemon essences or other gold-colored oils. Also, gold or yellow is the best color to use if you wish to cast a spell to contact spirit guides. Finally, you can use it to conjure happiness and harmony in your home.

Green

- **Element:** Earth
- **Chakra:** Heart
- **Astrological Sign:** Virgo
- **Energy:** Feminine

Green is used to invoke growth, promise, and hope. It is a symbol of love and vow renewals and is also used for workings related to health, healing, and tranquility. Suppose you are an Earth magic practitioner or Green witch. In that case, you can use this symbolic color to summon the Green Man, Gaia, and other Earth deities.

You may also use the color Green to channel the earth and its energies. This color is commonly used in money, abundance, and prosperity spells. Suppose you wish to get someone to assist you with something. In such instances, you can utilize green to emit a "green glow" that will pull them towards you.

If you're planning for a raise at work or meeting with a prospective investor, wear green textiles. Virgo is the astrological sign of the Green color. If your birthday falls between August 23rd and September 22nd, you're a Virgo – meaning that green could be your power color. Green has always been associated with growth, and Virgo is tied to agriculture and fresh life. It is, therefore, no surprise that green is Virgo's power color. When it comes to the color green, its representation is more important than the specific hue shade.

Blue

- **Element:** Water
- **Chakra:** Throat
- **Astrological Sign:** Libra
- **Energy:** Masculine

Blue represents peace, joy, and truth. Its shades have different meanings, but they all have a resonating theme. The color blue is associated with the water element and represents increased self-confidence and the capacity to reconcile the ordinary and spiritual aspects of life, among other things. A lighter shade of blue represents calm, gentility, understanding, tranquility, patience, understanding, wisdom, good fortune, etc. On the other hand, darker blue represents protection, reassurance, impulsivity, depression, changeability, and spiritual inspiration.

Blue is the color you go to when you wish to harness the elemental powers of the water and sky. You can use blue to invoke the water spirits of the Atlantis seas. In magical workings, blue is often used to summon cleansing and purification energy which comes from water.

To invite the spirits of calm and tranquility, many witches utilize blue in blessing rituals and ceremonies. Blue provides you with a road to uncovering the truth about your magical workings and spells. Libra is the associated astrological sign of the blue color. If you were born between September 23rd and October 22nd, you're a Libra, and blue is your color. As previously noted, cooler colors like green have physiological impacts. It is safe to say that blue is the coolest of all the cool colors. It is a soothing color with a proven ability to lower blood pressure and decrease heart rate. You can use it to instill an instant sense of calm amid stress.

As a result, blue has become the color of serenity, hope, and dependability. Many people see it as an "honest" hue since it exudes reliability and integrity. Lighter blue is often regarded as the perfect Libra power color. Still, again, shade isn't as important as representation and symbolism.

Black

- **Element:** Water

- **Chakra:** Root

- **Astrological Sign:** Scorpio

- **Energy:** Feminine

Black connotes negativity more than positivity to many people. It is the hue of melancholy, depression, grief, and mourning in many cultures. Many people also regard it to be a powerful and forceful color, which is why it can be perceived as abrasive sometimes.

Despite this, many people associate black with strength, authority, and influence. Because it was the hue of lush, fertile soil, ancient Egyptians regarded it as the color of life. It was only later that the hue began to earn its dreadful reputation.

In the world of witchcraft, black symbolizes protection, wisdom, grounding, dream work, banishing, and introspection. Some witches might say it represents discord, loss, evil, binding, shapeshifting, and repelling negativity. However, this primarily borders on perspective.

Nonetheless, black is one of the colors of Scorpio – the astrological sign for those born between October 23rd and November 21st. It is a sophisticated and beautiful hue that may provide a feeling of mystery elegance to a memorable event.

Black is regarded as the combination of all other colors. Therefore, you may use it in just about any spell, particularly ones related to protection, grounding, and binding.

Purple

- **Element:** Fire

- **Chakra:** Brow

- **Astrological Sign:** Sagittarius

- **Energy:** Masculine

Purple is widely regarded as the color of royalty, wisdom, and mystery. Spirituality, fantasy, and premonition are also related to it. Purple can fire up your creativity and lend new vitality to everyday encounters, whether it is in a rich royal tint or a softer lavender tone.

On the downside, this color is also associated with sensitivity and immaturity. Otherwise, it has a rich history of intrigue and luxury. It is considered to be linked to a higher plane of existence.

If you were born between November 22nd and December 21st, you're a Sagittarius, meaning purple is one of your colors. It means that you can use it in spells successfully, alongside plum and dark blue, other Sagittarius colors.

Purple and violet signify your spiritual connection, while lilac represents your vivacious inner child. All shades of this color inspire authority, leadership, and spirituality. They also support benevolence, humility, and a continual relationship with your deity (god-goddess).

You can use purple in spell work relating to influencing influential people, improving psychic abilities and spiritual powers, accessing hidden knowledge, and enhancing business progress. There are other kinds of spells to use it in, and you'll learn more as you progress.

Brown

- **Element:** Earth
- **Chakra:** Root
- **Astrological Sign:** Capricorn
- **Energy:** Feminine

Brown is the earth's color. It is fertile, nurturing, comforting, and stable. It offers a sense of relaxation and calm to those who adorn it. If you've ever paid attention to the color, you have likely noticed that it makes one feel cozy, warm, and safe.

This color symbolizes grounding, reliability, healing, elegance, sophistication, home, and other earthly qualities. As common with other earthy tones, foundation and grounding are associated with brown. Many people view brown as a bland and "boring" color, but how can it be when it is one of the Capricorn colors? Capricorn is anything but boring. If you were born between December 22nd and January 19th, you're a Capricorn. Brown symbolizes wisdom, strength, and an innate ability to withstand adversity. People with brown as their astrological color have a strong tendency to outlast tests of time.

Brown is frequently used by witches to indicate maturity and acute intelligence. It was prized by ancient peoples for the same reason as black: its earthy tones indicate growth and rebirth. Capricorn is an earth sign, which explains why brown is one of the most potent colors in magic.

Brown is also connected with unwavering commitment and a strong moral foundation. It is commonly employed in spells involving family and the strict moral code that distinguishes Capricorns from the rest of the world.

Indigo

- **Element:** Fire
- **Chakra:** Third eye
- **Astrological Sign:** Aquarius
- **Energy:** Masculine

Indigo is a color that represents honesty, integrity, and spirituality. It depicts the witches' family, ancestors, habits, and traditions. The hue also has a divinatory energy correlation, which means it may be utilized for prophecy. This color may be used to conjure cosmic forces and midnight energy. Intriguingly, indigo is the mystical hue correspondence of the inner mind and the Akashic records, which include all memories, acts, and events from the past, present, and future. To tap into the psychic world and maybe acquire telepathic skills, incorporate indigo into your knot magic work. Thoughts travel as quickly as you conceive them in the cosmos, to anywhere in the universe, and this is one power you can tap into with indigo magic.

Indigo is one of the Aquarius' colors, alongside white, turquoise, aquamarine, and bright gold. Suppose you were born between January 20th and February 18th. In that case, you're an Aquarius - meaning that your zodiac color could be indigo or any of the others.

Of course, there are many other colors with magical correspondences that will be helpful in your practice of cord magic. As you advance in your practice, you'll learn more about the correspondences and meanings of other colors and how you may incorporate them in your rituals, spell works, etc.

Don't forget to combine and apply these colors as previously explained. Color meaning plays a vital role in healing, divination, and magic, so you should choose colors that reflect your moods, feelings, and innate desires for everything in your life.

These colors reflect your true feelings about yourself, which is why they're essential in your magical endeavors. Colors have profound psychic and spiritual meanings and can significantly affect your energies, vibrations, and others' perceptions of you.

Therefore, you must master the meanings of colors and learn to use them to affect your rituals, spell work, ceremonies, etc.

Now that you understand the symbolism of colors, especially in magic, you might want to take a good look at your home, office, and workspace. It might be time to make changes that match your astrological sign, current vibrations, and intentions. Consider it an adventure into a symbolic expression of your most authentic and best self.

Chapter 4: Timing Is Key

You should not randomly practice a cord magic spell since there are different things to consider. For instance, you need to consider the planetary and astrological influences. This chapter focuses on the aspect of timing when practicing cord magic. It starts by looking at the moon then focuses on each astrological planet.

The Moon

Since time immemorial, the moon has always been associated with our lives. Several faiths understand the significance of the moon's lunar cycle, which is used to mark calendars and determine when specific ceremonies should be performed. The moon, like the Sun, is made up of many gods and goddesses. The moon is also the subject of hundreds of stories in mythology. It goes through three main phases; waxing, full, and waning moon.

Witches know the power of the different moon phases since they have been using them for guidance, luck, courage, success, and to enhance their spell power. The moon also has a lot of power and impact on our life because it is the nearest celestial body to us. If you practice witchcraft, you should be aware that synchronizing your spells or rituals with the phases of the moon can increase the potency of your spells and rituals.

The moon goes through several phases, each with its own set of strength and energy. Depending on the moon phase when a spell is cast, it might be powerful or void. Therefore, it is vital to ensure that you cast the correct spell under the appropriate moon phase for excellent results. The following are the different moon phases and their implications for your magic spells.

New Moon Phase

The start of a lunar cycle is signaled by the new moon. During this period, you may notice several nights when the moon appears as if it has disappeared completely, but it will be hiding behind the sun. This is the ideal time to perform spells that will need intention. It is also the time to add a new prayer to your ritual or habit.

This is the time when you concentrate on your inner self and take the steps necessary to achieve your objectives. The new moon is perfect for divination, deconstructive magic, and beginning new endeavors. It is also the best phase for a candle ritual where you aim to let go of certain things while requesting something you want.

Waxing Moon

When the moon enters the waxing phase, it looks like a "C" facing backward. As it grows, it will be gathering its powers, and the goddess will be beginning her journey. This is an excellent moment to cast a spell focusing on self-improvement or self-discovery. If you plan well, this can be the right time to go ahead and schedule your entire month.

The waxing moon stage is appropriate for practicing attraction magic or other spells that can draw positive energy. Protective spells, attraction, healing, innate beauty, psychic work, self-improvement, success, abundance, luck, and friendship are all useful spells to consider. An intention spell is the most appropriate where you write your intent on paper to recite when you perform the ritual.

First Quarter Moon

The first quarter moon is similar to the third quarter moon in that it is only lit midway. The sun will be on the moon's side at this time; the quarter phase is great for taking stock of your surroundings, as well as a time for introspection.

You should also take advantage of this opportunity to celebrate your successes and accomplishments. It is a great time to start thinking about your full moon rituals as well. When the moon is in the first quarter stage, it allows you to see everything that needs changing in your life and make necessary adjustments. You may use the time to cast spells that will bring you whatever you desire. Growth, motivation, divination, success, and strength are some of the other sorts of magic you should consider trying out. You must reflect on your past experiences and correct your wrongs.

Waxing Gibbous Moon

The waxing Gibbous moon stage provides you with more energy and presents the best opportunity to push hard to achieve what you have been struggling to finish. The silver lining of the dark moon is visible, which symbolizes energy.

IMAGE by NASA Goddard Space Flight Cent
https://www.flickr.com/photos/gsfc/5837031188

During this period, any rituals you undertake should be focused on awareness and productivity. Although you may successfully carry out the rituals, you must examine both your internal and external emotions and observe how they are impacted by your environment, putting more refined attention into your goals. Concentrate on your goal and believe that the moon will help you achieve it. This is also time to focus on constructive magic and nurture what you have already started. If you're feeling down, the moon will boost your confidence and power.

When the moon is in this phase, the best time to cast a spell is between the hours of 10 and 11 p.m. It will aid you in summoning the night goddesses to help you with your work. Health, development, success, attractiveness, and inspiration are some of the other types of magic that are appropriate for this stage.

Full Moon

A full moon is easily recognized by almost everyone, and its phase is associated with fertility and love. It encourages you to simultaneously offer and accept love. A full moon provides the most effective magical energy for practicing pagans and Wiccans, and it is the optimum time to execute different manifestation spells. During this period, you can

also perform banishment rituals.

IMAGE by dobs1973 https://www.flickr.com/photos/dobo1973/22837469825

Because a full moon has immense energy that helps you to feed your powers, this phase is the optimum time to enhance your divination and psychic abilities. Most witches often view a full moon as all-purpose since various forms of magic can be performed during this time. These can be destructive or constructive rituals.

You should make use of the full moon's opportunity to eliminate negative influences from your life, perform divination, build protective spells, and cleanse your crystals and instruments. The full moon should be used for important life events that demand a significant boost or shift. Also, use this time to celebrate success and learn to accept the things that did not go your way since this gives you experience. During this period, high power will lead you, and the most appropriate magic you might want to use is that associated with love, healing, charging, spirituality, dreams, and psychic growth.

Waning Gibbous Moon

As its strength begins to diminish, the right side of the moon will darken. The goddess symbol in this stage is called the Crone, which symbolizes full wisdom. The withering is a reminder that death is inevitable in a cycle of life. You must accept yourself since the moon is losing energy. This is an excellent moment to undertake a ritual related to conquering challenges in your life. During this moment, take a few steps back and reflect on yourself. In order to define your objectives and ambitions for the following month, you must first identify challenges in your life.

IMAGE by Marco Hosaka https://www.flickr.com/photos/imarui/25294997066

Knot magic is of the most appropriate rituals to do at this time. It is vital to consider and reflect on different things that may be acting as obstacles blocking you from achieving your goals. The waning gibbons are expelling, purging, and abandoning curses and negativity. It is the most appropriate moment for the spells to come to fruition in various ways.

Waning Moon

At this point, the moon's strength has been depleted, and it is about to succumb to nature's cycle. Don't be discouraged if you didn't meet your objectives for the month. It is all about self-compassion and seeing oneself as a unique individual.

You should discharge negative energy and concentrate on other insecurities. When the moon is waning, banishing magic is more effective, and you utilize the moment to get rid of whatever is bothering you. This is also the moment to call it quits on friendships, relationships, and anything else you want to withdraw from. Make use of the opportunity to recharge, heal, and relax, as well as meditate and nourish oneself.

Dark Moon

The majority of people utilize this time to recover their magical abilities, but some embrace the dark energy that comes with it. Others will be looking for closure; the majority of magic rituals conducted at this time will be aimed at breaking toxic habits. During this phase of the moon, you should consider casting protective charms. Use blessed white coarse salt or black salt to do a short protection spell.

Sprinkle your home, windowsills, and doors with it. It will assist you in constructing barriers that will protect you from harmful energy attempting to enter your home. Ready-to-use oil can also assist you in casting your intended spells. The dark moon marks the end of the lunar cycle, which leads up to the new moon. It is the period for destructive magic, shadow work, divorce, hexes, preventing stalkers, additions, obstructions, binding, and banishing; it is connected to the goddess's evil side. The full moon has less potency than destructive magic. The black moon energies may be used for healing, inner work, releasing, and cleaning, and it is also a good time for divination and soul-searching. It is also time to replenish your energy, relax, and refresh before the onset of the next waxing phase. Magic related to closure is ideal during this phase when the moon is dark.

Planets and Timing of Magic

Astrological planets have a great influence on our personalities and life in general. They also play a significant role in magical practice, so you should use them for timing purposes. There are ten planets in the universe, including the Moon and the Sun. In magical work, the earth is not used for planetary energy, although it is very important, as this is where we practice all our spells, rituals, or magical work.

Three of the planets are called "modern," Neptune, Pluto, and Uranus. They are not commonly used in magic since they were discovered when the telescope was invented. Modern astrologers at times use these planets but not always, and they also move slowly around the sun. For this discussion of magic planets and timing, we focus on seven planets and a star, known before the advent of the telescope; the Sun, Moon, Venus, Mercury, Saturn, Mars, and Jupiter.

The Sun

The sun is the most important planet, which provides life, light, and warmth to the earth. It is energetic, stimulating, and acts as a father figure in whatever we do. The Sun is related to Sunday in mystical works, and it is used to represent wealth, joy, happiness, healing, leadership, ego, and power.

Mars

The planet derives its name from the Roman God of war and is active and represents fiery energy. Mars is often believed to be destructive, and it possesses energy that can be used violently. Sexual energy, force, struggle, mortality, competitiveness, adversity, and achievement are all governed by this planet. Fast action, lust, battle, endurance, leadership, and physical competitions are ruled by it as well.

Mercury

This planet governs all types of communication, and it is characterized by healing. Mercury's energy is unexpected and explosive. Intelligence, reason, awareness, rationality, perceptions, transmission, writing, and other forms of communication are all governed by it. It also has an impact on issues such as children, social contracts, siblings, travel, and transportation. Mercury is traditionally associated with learning, mental health, addictions, higher education, travel, perceptions, authors, artists, and poets.

Jupiter

Jupiter is a judge, legislator, and human benefactor. Prosperity, leisure time, growth, indulgence, optimism, opportunity, morality, higher education, luck, and philosophy are all ruled by it. The energy of this planet is efficient and organized, and it also promotes growth and regulates legal issues. Magical works for development, prosperity, expansion, money, business, and attracting greater value are all possible.

Venus

Venus is the Roman goddess of love. The planet is made up of a gentle but harmonious energy. Natural love, pleasure, attractiveness, art, and other associated domains are all governed by this planet.

Venus can be used for peace, love, beauty, healing, tenderness, protection, and pleasure rituals.

Saturn

Saturn's energy is sluggish but enduring. Discipline, structure, responsibility, objectives, professional possibilities, structure, time, wisdom, patience, and more are all governed by it. You can do rituals that include overcoming restrictions, barriers, endings, or death when you are under the control of Saturn.

How Do You Cast Spells?

Based on planetary influence, you need to know other critical elements like calculating planetary hours during the day and nighttime. Distinct planets are connected with different planetary hours. For instance, each hour is ruled by a specific planet, making the influence apparent. However, planetary hours cannot be equated to man-made 60-minute hours. The chart below shows how different planets influence magical spells.

Chart of Planetary Influences

Planet	Influences
Saturn	Long-term goals, career goals, protection
Jupiter	Wealth and prosperity, meditation, luck
Mars	Courage, passion, defensive spells
Sun	Sunday Success, happiness, healing, boosting physical energy, strength

Venus	Love, romantic relationships, beauty, domestic efforts
Mercury	Education, legal issues, communications, self-improvement, wisdom
Moon	Psychic abilities, gardening, emotions, fertility, family

Magical Timing: How to Choose the Right Day for Your Spell

Planetary magic is complex since it blends ancient cosmology, astrology, and celestial bits of intelligence to produce the best results. You cannot randomly perform magic since there are special days and times to cast spells. To receive the finest results, make sure your magical activity is aligned with the proper planetary ruler. The planetary rulership comprises each planet's designated seven days of the week. The days are further separated into planetary hours so you can execute your magic at the precise moment. Below is the ruling for each planet for the seven days and the suggested type of magic you can perform on each.

Sunday (The Sun)

The sun is the brightest, most benevolent, and life-giving body in the sky. As a result, Sunday should be reserved for your most daring and powerful spells. It symbolizes new beginnings marked by hope, prosperity, health, charisma, and popularity. The first day of the week must also help you raise your profile, make new friends, gain confidence and leadership.

Monday (The Moon)

The moon is in charge on Mondays; it is a strong day, but it is not the best day for casting spells. Instead, it may be used for self-reflection, imagination, and deception. Monday is a good day for dream traveling, trance work, scrying, and fertility and love charms, among other things. Water magic is the best since the moon controls the tide.

Tuesday (Mars)

This is the day for nastier spells if the nice ones fail to work. On this day, you can cast charms of ambition, sexual potency, ambition, and vengeance. You can also use the opportunity to cultivate strength.

Wednesday (Mercury)

Wednesday is an excellent day to work on the components of travel, study, luck, and commerce. Addressing y our communication, awareness, and attention should be your main priority. It is also a good day for making money drawing charms, divination using runes, cards, or lots. If you want to perform a spell to mislead or distract, Wednesday is the appropriate day.

Thursday (Jupiter)

Thursday is the finest day to cast spells for good health, success, and fortune. Mercury can bring quick cash, so you can consider signing a contract to get property. Visualize future success, bless family, friends, and home on Thursdays.

Friday (Venus)

Friday is associated with love magic; it is customary to do draw charms to draw your beloved closer. Friday is also a day for friendship, reconciliation, sympathy, and self-love. You can pick herbs and plants for magical use on Friday since Venus is tied to the natural world. Try out some pleasure and delight spells.

Saturday (Saturn)

Saturn rules the last day of the week, and it may be utilized for banishment and binding spells. Saturday is also ideal for communicating with your ancestors and other spirits through underworld magic. Souls who have died naturally should be remembered on Saturday, whereas heroes should be honored on Tuesday. Saturn's energy aids in the development of knowledge and patience. You must strive to overcome addiction and visit elders to reflect on the past on Saturdays.

Planetary Hours

Each day of the week is further divided into planetary hours that can be ruled by the same planet or different. These hours can be used differently, so you must choose the appropriate days for specific spells. You can also consult professional magicians for the correct planetary hours. You also need to understand how the hours apply to the specific time of day and spells you want to perform. However, it is better to do some work at the wrong time than throw away the magic. When planetary timing, the options that determine the outcomes of spell work differ, so try it to see how timing works.

It can be noted that there is an excellent link between magic and planetary influences, meaning that you cannot randomly practice your spell work since many things must first be considered. When practicing cord magic, you need to ensure good timing, and you can achieve this by taking into account different astrological elements. The appropriate time is essential to practice certain spells or rituals.

Chapter 5: Knots and Numerology

Every day, you think about numbers from the moment you wake. What time is it? How many miles should you run? How much will the new apartment cost? Is it time to celebrate someone's birthday? What is the date?

The argument is that numbers are important in our daily lives and help to interpret a variety of situations. We use them to organize our ideas, our reality, and our everyday lives. As a result, they've always been an integral part of our lives. Math, which is a global language, would not exist without numbers. There would be no way to solve many universal mysteries, and human history would remain lost to us. After all, how would we communicate important dates without numbers?

Numbers connote many things across different cultures. Humans rely on the tested-and-true symbolism of specific numbers. Gamblers, for example, frequently place bets on the number seven since it is thought to bring luck.

Because the words for death and four are too close in the Chinese language, several Chinese hotels refuse to count a fourth level. Similarly, m Many hotels across the globe do not skip the thirteenth floor since the number 13 is considered unlucky, associated with death and misery. Furthermore, Christians consider the number "666" to be the antichrist's number, and it is frequently represented in horror films to alarm audiences. Because numbers play such an important role in our daily lives, their significance is naturally reflected in the realms of magic, witchcraft, and the occult as well. Many parts of witchcraft include numbers, to the point that numbers have become an integral part of magic, as significant as anything else. To put it another way, number magic exists just like color magic or any other type of magic. It isn't random when a witch adds five crystals in a spell or chants an incantation three times or sets up five candles for a ritual. The numbers are significant to the ritual and its objective.

You use specific numbers because of their symbolism in the occult and what they represent to you. This chapter is about the power of numbers and why they're essential in knot magic, as well as any other magic. The goal is to illustrate how you can channel the magic of numbers to enhance your witchcraft. More than anything, numbers are significant in knot magic.

Numerology helps you understand the energy surrounding every aspect of life, and it sheds meaning in life's path and destiny via numbers. Everything that arises from creation can be represented numerically or mathematically. The system is completely self-contained, consistent, and uncompromised. Mathematics can explain everything in the cosmos, from planetary motions to gravity to how objects float on water. Many people consider math a spiritual mysticism disguised, and numerology as the "mystical study" of numeric meanings and their external influence." Pythagoras, a Greek philosopher, thought that numbers generate energies that make up our physical plane. One of the most amazing things about math is that it is unaffected by societal change, cultural change, or new technologies. Numbers are unchanging, incorruptible, and cohesive - they characterize all spatial relations with uncanny accuracy. The spiritual plane is translated into physical formulae through mathematics, forming an organic link between both mystical and material planes. Numbers are the letters of the mathematical language, and we have ten numbers that comprise all numbers that exist in the universe. From 1 - 9, each number is embedded with unique energy through which it offers vital insight into existence's greater purpose.

Each number is a magical building block that defines logic in a relatable way. Together, the relationship between these numbers embodies the collective and cumulative universe. They each represent a human's purpose as well as their spiritual and romantic life. This is the essence of numerology.

Numerology can help you understand your relationships, career, business, family life, health, spirituality, and personality. All of these can be mathematically understood and even modified with the proper knowledge.

Many people think that a person's fate is determined by the day and hour of their birth. The reverse is true: you choose when you'll be born, even before you're born, knowing deep down in your spirit the ideal numerological day and time for your birth. In other words, you select your destiny and associated day and time, as well as your numerology, which includes your destiny number and life path number. Numerology exists to remind you of your chosen life path, much as astrology uses the planets and zodiac signs to provide insight into your personality and life path as well. It teaches you the hidden symbolism of numbers and the impact they hold on to your life.

You can understand the universe and your destiny by integrating your magical practices with numerology. The aim is to use the energies and vibrations of numbers in your birth date, given name, and even your address to uncover the secrets behind a fulfilled life; for yourself, your loved ones, and others.

Numerology is prevalent throughout a wide range of cultures, including the Greeks, Egyptians, and Incans. Whatever the cultural context, all numerological systems employ numbers to explain old riddles and important life concerns, such as purpose or being. Keep in mind that numerology systems are interpreted differently in each culture. We'll talk about how various civilizations have their own unique details when it comes to numerology. However, the focus here is on Western numerology and how you can integrate it with knot magic to amplify the potency of your spells, rituals, and magical workings.

Chaldean Numerology

Chaldean numerology is concerned with both single numbers (1-9) and complex numerals. Single numbers derived from a person's name were used to focus on superficial personality traits. Double numerals, on the other hand, had more mystical significance.

1	2	3	4	5	6	7	8	9
A	B	C	D	E	F	G	H	I
J	K	L	M	N	O	P	Q	R
S	T	U	V	W	X	Y	Z	

Modern-day numerology charts are based upon the Pythagorean system.

The numerologist studies the date of birth after the person's name has been shortened in Chaldean numerology. This was deemed more significant since it served as a marker of the individual's historical position. Even if you change your name, your birth date and associated number stay the same. Chaldean numerology has 52 number correspondences. In comparison to Western numerology, below are the meanings of 1-9, 11, 22, and 33.

- **1 – The Sacred Masculine:** Individuality, self-awareness, purpose, and dominance. Represented by The Mage in the Tarot systems.

- **2 – The Sacred Feminine:** Duality, partnership, caution, cooperation, and decision-making. In the Tarot, the High Priestess represents her.

- **3 – The Power of Manifestation:** Artistry, romance, joy, energy. Represented by the Empress in the Tarot.

- **4 – Conscious Self:** Earth energies, safety, stability, and the rule of law. In the Tarot, The Emperor represents consciousness.

- **5 – The Bard:** Sexuality, flexibility, adventure, communication, and liberty. In the Tarot, the Hierophant represents the bard.

- **6 – The Healer:** Harmony, symmetry, loyalty, love, and sound advice. In the Tarot, this is represented by the Lovers Card.

- **7 – The Mysteries:** The Metaphysical, spirituality, yearning, and introspection. In the Tarot, these are represented by The Chariot.

- **8 – The Constant Universal Energy:** Control, power, awareness, and recognition of fair labor. In the Tarot, it is represented by the Justice Card.

- **9 – The Humanitarian:** Compassion, generosity, progress, patience, and acceptance. In the Tarot, it is represented by The Hermit.

- **11 – The Warning:** Personal hardships, adversity, unanticipated danger, deception, and treachery.

- **22 – The Illusion:** False hopes and judgments, dreams without foundation.

• **33 – The Promise:** Help gained through love and honesty.

Chinese Numerology

Chinese numerology depends on how numbers sound when pronounced out loud. Each number contains either good or negative traits, serving as a foundation on which you may create your particular number's energies with assurance. The digits have elemental meanings as well.

LUCKY NUMBERS

Numbers have special meaning in Chinese culture for phonetic reasons. Numbers spoken in the languages of both Mandarin and Cantonese have homonyms that can denote luck, often good but sometimes bad. Here is how Chinese associate the numbers one through nine, according to their pronunciation in Mandarin.

DEFINITION OF HOHONYM	MANDARIN PRONUNCIATION	WRITTEN IN SIMPLIFIED CHINESE	NUMBER
together, want	yi	一	1
love, easy	er	二	2
earn, live	san	三	3
death	si	四	4
me, not	wu	五	5
Smooth	liu	六	6
together	qi	七	7
fortune, wealth	ba	八	8
long time	jiu	九	9

Source: WSJ research

• **One:** Is the water element, representing a level of independence that borders on extreme loneliness.

• **Two:** Is of the Earth element, representing willpower and good fortune.

• **Three:** Is of the wood element, representing creativity and abundance.

• **Four:** Is of the wood element, representing misfortune and may portend death.

- **Five:** Is of the earth element but tied to all five natural elements. It is a balance between the numbers.

- **Six:** Is of the metal element, linked to auspicious vibrations and may represent wealth.

- **Seven:** Is of the metal element, representing positive relationships.

- **Eight:** Is of the earth element, representing wealth, prosperity, and success.

- **Nine:** Is of the fire element, representing truth, leadership, and longevity.

Indian Numerology

Indian numerology system operates on assigning three critical numbers to a person. The first is the psychic number, which represents talents and fundamental character. This one is extracted from the day of the month you were born.

The second number is your destiny number, which represents how the rest of the world sees you and how karma affects your life. Comparable to the Pythagorean numerological system's life path number, it is derived from the sum of your birth date, month, and year. Finally, we have a third, the name number. This one is all about how you interact with other people. Assume you switch your name or find yourself being referred to with new nicknames. In that case, the vibrations with which you work change according to these names and nicknames. Each letter in your name corresponds to a numerical value.

Here are the numbers and associated attributes:

- **1 – The Sun:** Fame, courage, vital energy.

- **2 – The Moon:** Gentle disposition, intelligence, travel.

- **3 – Virtue:** Trustworthiness, respect, justice.

- **4 – The Occult:** Power, magic, psychic ability.

- **5 – Money:** Financial stability, communication skills, a keen mind.

- **6 – Beauty:** Perfection, music, sports, artistic practice.

- **7 – The Sage:** Metaphysical sciences and healing arts.

- **8 – Loyalty:** Lengthy life span, perseverance, improvement through honest work.

- **9 – Consistency:** Perseverance, fortitude, physical prowess, and independence.

Number	Planet	Alphabet
1	Sun	A I J Q Y
2	Moon	B K R
3	Jupiter	C G L S
4	Rahu Uranus	D M T
5	Mercury	E H N X
6	Venus	U V W
7	Ketu Neptune	O Z
8	Saturn	P F
9	Mars	No Alphabet

Above is a chart that shows the associations between letters and numbers and how to determine a name number.

Pythagorean Numerology

The Pythagorean numerology system is the most well-known and commonly recognized method of dealing with numbers and symbols. Pythagoras collected cues from varying mathematical disciplines and spiritual influences from the Masons, Rosicrucian, and Druids. He viewed the world uniquely.

He believed that "numbers rule the universe." He also believed in the Wiccan ideal to "know thyself." According to Pythagoras, we must understand ourselves to understand God and the Universe.

Pythagorean numerology is primarily concerned with the numbers 1 through 9 and a person's birth date. It is rather simple to reduce this to a single digit. For instance, 8/21/95 is 8+2+1+1+9+9+5 = 35 and 3+5 = 8. This is how you get a person's life path number.

If the result is 11, 22, or 33, however, you do not subtract from the addition. These are master figures, which represent higher levels of consciousness and achievement. The number 11 represents the messenger, the number 22 the teacher, and the number 33 the leader or sage. The life path number is singlehandedly regarded as the most critical numeral in a person's entire numerological outlook. It offers information about personality qualities, adversities, and problems to come, as well as life lessons to be learned.

The Heart's Desire Number and the numerical correspondences with the letters in an individual's entire given birth name are used to calculate the personality number. The HDN is obtained from the vowels in the person's given name.

Western Numerology

The best thing about knowing different approaches to numerology is that it gives you a level of versatility that isn't available to the average witch. Below is a comparison of the previously explained numerological systems with the Western system and the symbolic value attributed to single and compound numbers.

One

E Pluribus Unum. Creation. The beginning. Coming out in first place in everything you do is obviously symbolized by the number one. It denotes great leadership qualities, charm, and an intrinsic capacity to inspire followership from those around you in the workplace.

In relationships and matters of love, it means you can survive on your own without loneliness. You may enjoy being in a relationship, but you also love and value your individuality – sometimes to a fault.

In witchcraft, one represents intention. You use it to emphasize your intention and its importance.

If a specific date adds up to number one for you, make it a point to begin new initiatives, go on a first date, or make plans for the future on that day.

Two

The world appears divided into two. Sun and moon, night and day, light and dark, life and death, earth and sea are all examples of opposites and balance. There is duality everywhere you look. Two is the number of knowledge. It represents the Sacred Feminine and embodies nurture, insight, love, kindness, endurance, diplomacy.

Two means you thrive in harmony. Your relationships thrive – friendship, family, romantic relationships, coworkers, etc. If your life path number is two, it means you're honest and down to earth, and everyone enjoys your company.

However, it also means that maintaining harmony is so important to you that you might forgo your individuality, neglect boundaries, and make sacrifices that others might not be willing to reciprocate.

Two is an excellent number for partnership in matters of business. If the sum of a specific date adds up to two, that means you're better off making business deals through partnership and teamwork.

Three

Three is a lucky number. It is very important in many faiths across the world. It symbolizes the past, present, and future. In some cultures and faiths, three elements of God combine to form a whole, known as a trinity. The Triple Goddess, for example, consists of a maiden, a mother, and a crone. Many people think that the world is split into three parts: heaven, earth, and hell. When we narrate the stories of our lives, there is always a beginning, middle, and end. Every color is made up of three main colors; three wishes are granted by Genies. Humans do not hear evil, speak evil, or see evil – a triangle is one of the shapes that creates a mystical connection between the three. Witches frequently repeat spells and incantations three times.

Three indicates a whole spell cycle in magic and witchcraft. You started by sending an intention. Then you cast the magic, and the spell's goal is achieved. The idea here, once again, is that three is a mystical number. It symbolizes sociality, self-expression, generosity, fun, and collaboration – but not in the same way that two does. Suppose your life path number is three. In that case, everyone likes to be around you – most likely because you're a fun party animal!

This also means you tend to pursue shallow things over deeper, more meaningful ones. In love matters, you are inclined to have more than one partner at a time. You may find commitment difficult and very unsettling. But once you make the decision to commit, you should do it well. If the total of a given day equals three, it indicates that you should consider gathering friends and loved ones, socializing, and letting go. In other words, that date is a beautiful time to enjoy yourself.

Four

The number four represents the four cardinal points, seasons, and elements; north, south, east, and west, and earth, air, fire, and water. Spring, summer, winter, and fall. In the witchcraft community, there is the legend of Four Thieves of Vinegar.

The four horsemen of the apocalypse are Death, Famine, War, and Conquest. The four noble truths are found in Buddhism, while the cross has four points in Christianity. Because of its relationship with the cardinal points, seasons, and elements, the number four is ideal for any magical activity incorporating any of these. Suppose your life path number is four. In that case, you're an administrative and organized person on whom many can depend. You have a talent for developing, implementing, and executing enormous projects, which you can potentially grow to become even larger.

In every circumstance, you can notice the small details as well as the broad image. It is critical to date individuals who are as talented and efficient as you are. Otherwise, you'll always find yourself in charge of everything, which may not make you feel good. In a relationship, there's an overwhelming tendency to feel like the parent.

If the sum of a specific date adds up to four, it is a perfect day to implement tasks and generally make things happen.

Five

Five is significantly associated with marriage. It symbolized humanity and is especially important in witchcraft. When stretched, the five conspicuous appendages form a star (pentacle). Humans have five senses and five fingers and toes.

The classic rose has five petals and is a hidden emblem of the occult language. The number 5 is symbolized in Middle Eastern cultures by the Hamsa hand and is thought to shield individuals from the evil eye. In elemental magic, the witch (you) represents the fifth element, which is the soul. It provides the additional spark required to concentrate on the magic being done. Five recognizes that humans are divinely inspired and capable of incredible things. Due to this, five is a magical number.

If your life path number is five, it makes you a free and independent spirit with a penchant for travel and adventure. You want a life that's as flexible as possible and may prefer to live from country to country – immersing in different experiences, languages, and cultures.

In love matters, you may shy entirely away from partners if you cannot find someone that's as free-spirited as you. You want your equal – someone who's willing to travel the world alongside you and open to new adventures.

If the digit of a specific date sums up to five, it means that day, week, or month is an excellent time to try something new.

Six

Six is associated with healing – physical, emotional, and spiritual. It is the number of responsibilities and refers to people who are compassionate, understanding, devoted, accountable, and caring.

You think, talk, and act from your heart if your life path number is six. You're warm, affectionate, and true in your love. You flourish in occupations and settings that allow you to put your great talents to use, such as teaching, therapy, social work, or being a pediatrician. This score indicates that you are well-suited to long-term relationships and family life. You don't have a strong desire for superficial romantic relationships. If a connection is formed between you and someone, it is most likely a genuine one. However, you may find that you focus too much on your relationships – which makes you a magnet for individuals who can't care as much as you do.

If the sum of a date adds up to six, it makes it a wonderful day to find love. You can also use that day, week, or month to implement a universal theme and help less-privileged people in distant communities. Generally, it is an excellent time to be there for others without neglecting your own needs and wants.

Seven

Seven is a spiritual number. It is the number of systematic, intelligent, refined, focused, insightful, thoughtful, and courteous people. Those having the number seven for their life path are mostly impacted by their intellect.

If you're one of these folks, you could find yourself drawn to spiritual or meditation practices, as well as philosophical discussions. You'd be fantastic as a guru, philosopher, or lecturer. However, being overly focused on your thoughts might make things of the heart difficult to handle. In other words, romantic interactions may be more difficult for you than usual, owing to your inability to pick up on or convey hints. You don't communicate your feelings that well, and you may blame your spouse for being too emotional and frantic - which may be a natural reaction. If the total of two dates equals seven, it is a good time to come up with fresh ideas, write, or meditate.

Eight

Eight is the authority figure among the numbers. It is the number of leadership, success, symmetry, sound judgment, talent, and effectiveness. The number eight pushes one to be motivated and hardworking, indicating that you'd be capable of completing tasks.

Suppose eight is your life path number. In that case, you have a knack for being on top of your finances. You're great at budgeting, saving, and investing. Career paths you would thrive in include funds manager, investment advisor, etc.

You're excellent at methodical and numerical thinking, but that makes love and relationships difficult. You must put this thinking aside if you wish to fall in love and have a successful relationship. If you let go, you'll find love or vice versa.

If the sum of a date adds up to eight, it makes it an excellent day or time to make plans, execute your to-do list, and generally work on the logic behind the things you want.

Nine

Nine embodies generosity, refinement, nobility, kindness, gentility, etc. This number strengthens your belief in humanity. If you have the number nine as your life path number, you most likely feel that all humans are equal in essence and that religion and race should not be used to divide – but to unite.

You're a natural leader who might easily lead a non-profit. However, you may not be placing enough limits on your giving. For example, you could give away your single sweater, oblivious to the fact that this would leave you chilly later. You may find it difficult to prioritize yourself in relationships. Recognize that there is a limit to how much you can give. Always attend to your needs, no matter how trivial they may seem compared to others' needs.

As previously noted, 11, 22, and 33 are considered the strongest numbers in the numerology chart.

Now, you may be wondering how to apply the symbolism and meanings of these numbers to knot magic or any other kind of magic. As made evident so far, numbers are of particular importance in knot magic. They are at the center of everything.

You don't just tie a random number of knots in a spell unless it aligns with your goal. Numbers mean something, and it is important to remember this as you explore and progress in knot magic.

The Use of Numbers in Knot Magic

While learning about your personality, life path, and fate through numbers is certainly useful, you can accomplish a lot more with these numbers if you incorporate them well enough into your magical practice. For example, suppose you wish to perform a goddess-oriented ritual to honor the mother, maiden, crone, witches, etc. In that case, the most suitable number for this would be 2 – because it symbolizes divine femininity.

Keeping this in mind, you can:

- Set two candles at the quarter points. In other words, two each to the north, south, east, and west.

- Use foods that are goddess-oriented, similar to how a Kitchen witch would.

- Add two symbolic items inside your magic pouches.

- Use two defining components in your charms and spells.

- Recite your spell or invocation twice.

- Do the ritual on a date with two as a key number

The above is just a general example of how numbers can be symbolically applied in magic. In ritual and magic, keep in mind that each element contributes to and affects the greater details and significance of what you're doing. Extra care with these details is the surest way to strengthen the results of any spell or ritual.

Below is a more comprehensive idea relating to knotwork for numbers 1-5, the most commonly used in knotwork.

- **One:** Invoke the number one in a knot spell focused on a group, such as family. For example, you can tie one knot each for every member of the family for harmony. Alternatively, you can set your intention with one knot or one crystal in your knotwork.

Another way is to represent each family member with one symbol. Then, you can burn one white candle and make your intention for the group known. After this minimalist spell is completed, you can knot or braid each symbol into one (single) cord and hang it in a conspicuous location.

- **Two:** Invoke the number two for spells aimed at bonding two things together, physically or mentally. Find something to represent what you'd like to bond appropriately. Burn two candles for two hours and let the wax melt over the two symbolic pieces. Now, tie the two pieces into separate cords and braid them together.

You can repeat this process twice. When the moon is in its second phase, or on the second day of the week, cast your magic. During the knotwork, use a mirror to mimic every action through your reflection if you're the spell's focus.

- **Three:** Tie a knot of three when you're trying to meet a goal but confused on how to reach the outcome. Work backward to figure out how to reach the middle and visualize your goal as a story. Concentrate on spots that are particularly hard to knot and consider breaking further into three. You'll come to realize that both life problems and magic are easier to understand when you break them down into three parts.

- **Four:** Create a knot spell for the beginning of each season by setting an appropriate intention for the time. Assign different elements to channel for strength during difficult times. You can even do the Four Thieves vinegar that was briefly mentioned. It is a protective concoction that you can sprinkle at the entrance of your home every quarter of the month.

- **Five:** As you've learned, you're the most important of any spell you cast. Without you, magic, rituals, and spells mean nothing. Immerse yourself in all magical workings. Believe and accept. Set your goal and make your intention known.

There's also something called the personal number in numerology and witchcraft. Everyone has a specific number that means something to them. Your personal number is unique to you. You can incorporate this number in all kinds of spells, particularly those centered on you.

When you do magic without a lot of extras, this number should represent you. It is your secret ingredient, the key to personalizing your spells and workings. Inscribe this number on a concealed portion of your body or write it down to give it strength. Remember to keep the number a secret and not reveal it to anybody else. You should be the only one who understands what it means and why it is special to you. When you need a boost in your magical task, use and channel the power you've saved up from your number.

Chapter 6: The Knotwork Process

The knotwork process involves setting an intention and the knotting itself. Much of this chapter focuses on how to set intentions into your cords effectively. After all, that is the most important part of any magical activity.

https://unsplash.com/photos/red-rope-on-three-branch-St4qInZrYC4

Your intention is the energy you send into the knots – it creates the magic. However, you'll also find vital information on basic preparation steps for any magical work.

Naturally, there are certain things to do before the knotwork itself. Regardless of your witchcraft path, it is essential to prepare yourself before any magical activity. It is a crucial part of the process.

Your preparation doesn't have to be complex or elaborate. The essential thing is to set up the sacred space for the spell work or ritual, and most importantly, you must prepare yourself. Not all witches practice in similar ways. So, be open to experimenting with preparation to explore what works for you and what doesn't.

Cleansing

Cleansing yourself with a clean bath is the first step in preparation. Take considerable time to clean yourself thoroughly in a salt or herbal bath. You may also clean up with a special soap. It is not compulsory to do the cleansing right before the work – the time is your choice to make. Some witches do it the night before, based on what works for their lifestyle and schedule.

You may ornament your cleaning rituals with candles, crystals, and essential oils. But be careful with how you handle crystals around water. Some crystals and gemstones aren't meant to contact saltwater or any other kind of water at that. Ensure you do some research to ascertain that a particular crystal is safe to use during the ritual bath.

Consecrate the Sacred Space

Start by sweeping or vacuuming the room where your knotwork will take place. Then, use a bundle of sage to smudge and cleanse the energies around the room. Clean yourself and anyone else participating in the knotwork or spellcasting with the smudge herbs.

Sound is also quite effective at consecrating and ridding a space of negative energies. Use a bell, rattle, drum, or chime to eliminate negative energy from the sacred space and call in the positive energy.

Wear Colors That Align with the Spell's Goal

As you've learned, color energy is a vital aspect of knotwork and spellcasting. Choose clothing and adornment that match the energy you want to invite into the sacred space and your goal. Refer back to chapter three to choose colors that match what you need. For example, if the knotwork is for money spells, then you might want to add plenty of green to the environment.

Cast a Circle

Casting a circle is the equivalent of creating a boundary – ensuring that only the energies you invite can enter the space you occupy. You can cast the circle in meditation or simply trace out circle edges in the space using an athame. Other ways include marking the boundary with oils, salt, or blessed water.

Once you've done the above, it is time to start the knotwork process. So, how do you set intentions that are sure to make your spell successful?

Setting Intentions into the Cords

If you aren't new to the witchcraft community, you must know that "intention" is something of a buzzword. While many witches may throw it around carelessly, you should know that intention is single-handedly the most important aspect of magical working.

The question is, what is intention? How and when do you use it? Simplifying this concept is the key to ensuring you know what the knotwork process entails.

Setting the intention is the process of clearly communicating your wish, desire, needs, and wants to the universe, deities, spirits, etc. When an Earth witch performs a spell, their intention is known to nature, Gaia, the Green man, etc.

Cord magic does not require you to set intentions for a specific spirit or deity. Your intention is usually carried into the universe. Still, this doesn't mean you can't incorporate elements of other magic forms into cord magic.

For example, you can do a simple knotwork with the intention addressed to the Earth or Gaia – especially if the knotwork is targeted at something relevant to nature.

In witchcraft, the intention is the foundation of spells and rituals. Setting the right intention gets you what you want. In contrast, an unclear or wrong intention inhibits your spell from producing the desired results.

In witchcraft, a spell focuses intention on a specific goal or action. It consecrates all your personal energies into the intention so that you can clearly articulate what you need to the universe.

Imagine a world where you perform magic without intention. How does one perform a money spell without articulating the need for money? The intention is the core of magic and witchcraft.

Before setting an intention, be certain you know precisely what you want. You'll only get imprecise and uncertain results if you don't clearly articulate your wants or needs. It is best to be as specific as possible – you can even add time constraints.

For example, suppose you want enough money to buy a new house. The first intention that naturally conceives in your mind is "I want to buy a nice, new house."

The problem with the above is that you're just expressing a want to the universe. You aren't demanding for the universe to act, so you'll get nothing more than wanting back – first rule: Make your intention like you already have what you seek.

Another problem is that there is no specified time in that intention. Not telling the universe when you want what you want leaves it open to discretion – you might get it in a millisecond or ten years. So, be specific with the timeframe to ensure the spell works for as long as you need it to. Once you no longer need that thing, the spell will naturally dissipate.

The last problematic thing in that intention is what you're asking for. It is normal to want to live in a nice house, but intentions should always be set within reasonable limits. This is particularly important if you're new to witchcraft and intention setting. Always stick to reasonably attainable demands.

The above intention could be revised to look like:

> *"I wish to make enough money to save for a nice and comfortable home before my 30s."*

This intention does not carry hopes or wants. Instead, it sets what you need exactly. The timeframe ensures you have a reliable income that can fund that need for many years.

You'll like intention setting because it opens up the path to self-awareness, introspection, and meditation. To learn to cultivate genuinely beneficial intentions, you must reflect on your motives and seek a connection with your higher self. When you want to set an intention for a new spell, reflect and make sure you truly desire the result.

Below are the steps to set an intention.

Write

This is easily the simplest way to set forth your intention into the universe. Writing an intention down directs your focus and energy into the writing materials, feeling it flow from you into the pen and paper. Not only is this method satisfying and foolproof, but it is also the best choice for amateur witches. The point of writing is to know what to visualize exactly when you start your knotwork.

Before You Begin, Answer the Question: What actively obstructs me from making the things I want happen? This is a question that you might spend an entire afternoon pondering on. So, do this before preparing for the spellwork. Grab a journal, pen, and a pair of headphones and head to your favorite café.

Once Settled, Ask Yourself: What do I want? Set a timer to prevent your thoughts from running amok. Write down the first answer that comes to mind, even if it is absurd or trivial. For instance, assuming the spell you're about to do is regarding your relationship. In that case, list as many things as possible as you want in your ideal relationship.

Now, Answer the Question: Why don't I have the thing I want yet? Then, write down your limits and weaknesses. Find patterns that point to self-limiting tendencies.

By the end of this simple exercise, you must have achieved a multi-dimensional understanding of how you're obstructing your follow-through.

Of course, this doesn't mean your magical intention for a spell should focus on these limitations. Instead, it narrows down your vision so you know precisely what to visualize as you tie those knots into your cord.

Be Articulate

Magic has no syntax for intention phrasing, but you have to find a set of words that feel logically coherent. Find language and words that align with your innate feelings. Keep in mind that it is less about the words and more about the feelings they evoke.

A realistic and powerful intention penetrates your senses – meaning you can see, feel, and taste it. Always use "I" in setting an intention.

I want. I wish... I must... I will

Try distilling your intention into a 3-word mantra that you can recite as you tie your knots. You can even try syncing it with the melody of your favorite tune to get into the rhythm. Doing this will ensure that you feel the power of the intention before anything else.

Check with the Planets and Zodiacs

Don't forget or underestimate the influence of astrological bodies in magic. You need the moon and planets to activate your intentions. Check the charts and forecast to ascertain that your intention is compatible with the celestial energies you're manifesting it in.

https://pixabay.com/zh/vectors/zodiac-astrology-astronomy-5921179/

New witches often practice magic without considering the zodiac season and how it can dictate the result of their spells and rituals. However, as established in Chapter Four, timing (astrological climate) is significantly influential.

For instance, you can't fully activate the intentions for beauty, self-love, or relationships during the cycle after the Capricorn new moon. It is much better to set it as an intention in Libra, Leo, or Cancer vibes.

Thankfully, you don't need to be an astrologist to set effective magic intentions that align with the planets and zodiacs. Just follow the charts in Chapter Four.

Visualization

Visualization is a vital aspect of setting intention into the cords. While it is an abstract process, the skill is a must-have for any witch. Illustrate your intention in your mind's eye and see it manifesting in your life as you reap the benefits.

For instance, if your intention is "I want a nice house in my 30s," picture yourself in the future (30s) enjoying the view in your new home.

Not only does visualization solidify your intent, but it is also a foolproof way to ensure that the intention is accurate. Suppose you can vividly visualize the results of your intention, and it flows freely. In that case, it makes it accurate and more likely to manifest.

Suppose you can't picture it for some reason, or the outcome isn't vivid in your mind's eye. In that case, reflect on what you want and rethink the details.

Incorporate a Spell

You can set your intention with a spell or ritual, depending on what you want. Spells, rituals, and intentions are closely knitted because they naturally work together in the world of magic and witchcraft.

As previously explained, intention holds most of the power and energy in a spell because it is your way of communicating your desired result with the universe. Using a spell to set an intention is fundamental in witchcraft. It is a way to amplify the power of the intention.

Spells increase the specificity of your intention. So, if writing or visualizing isn't enough, you can take it a step further by incorporating a spell.

Now, this is where knotwork comes in. There are hundreds of spells to match different intentions. The key is to find credible ones. If you can find one that provides the results you seek, you can return to it time and time again.

The best thing is that you can create your own spells and rituals. Here's a good example of a money spell:

- Draw a symbol that represents financial stability

- Dress a green candle with oils and herbs that correspond with wealth

- Use a green cord for your spell

- Visualize your intention or recite it as you tie the knots until you reach the number that represents wealth

According to Indian numerology, eight represents wealth. So, tie eight knots into the cord and repeat your intention as you do this. As you complete each knot, recite each line below to reinforce your intention.

"By knot of one, the spell begins.

By knot of two, it becomes true

By knot of three, so shall it be

By knot of four, I store this power

By knot of five, the spell lives

By knot of six, I fix this spell

By knot of seven, it shall be fate

By knots of eight, what's done is mine."

The above is just an idea of how you might do a money knot spell. You can get creative and try different ingredients and tools. Nonetheless, ensure to research material before using it.

Below are the best materials to use in knotwork:

- Yarn
- Hemp
- Rope
- Embroidery thread

So, how do you jumpstart the knotwork process after setting an intention?

Essentially, you need to decide if you want to attract something or push it away. If you wish to push something away, you can burn the knotwork after braiding it. On the other hand, keep the knotwork nearby if you wish to draw something closer. The best thing about working magic is that you can discover what works best for you.

In subsequent chapters, you'll find more comprehensive examples of knot spells for different intentions.

Clearing Your Intention of Blocks

Setting an intention isn't enough – you must ensure nothing is blocking the intention from being fulfilled. Every negative thought, feeling, belief, and fear within you is a block meant to obstruct the manifestation of your intention.

Blocks are quite common in magical workings. They're tricky to notice or eliminate because they're rooted in the subconscious mind. It means you may not even realize the presence of a block when performing spells or rituals.

Fortunately, there are many ways to tell if you have blocks that need to be eliminated before a spell. A good way is to state your intention aloud and observe if any nagging feeling or thought accompanies it. So, take note of the thoughts and feelings that arise when you state an intent aloud.

Another way is to think about the current situation you're trying to address and write down all the good things about the situation.

For example, suppose you intend to attract a soul mate; in that case, note the benefits of being single. Think long and hard – no matter how bad it may seem, there's always an upside to any situation. It might seem trivial, *but it matters.*

As a single person, you might enjoy hanging out alone with other single friends. Now, examine that upside and determine if it is a potential block for your intention.

Pay attention to your feelings. Is there an intense feeling of worry that a new partner will affect your relationship with your single friends? If yes, encourage yourself to look at the situation from an entirely different perspective.

You could tell yourself that change is needed for growth. Or that your friends will be happy for you, regardless of your relationship status. This technique can also be used to work around seemingly bigger blocks.

Whether you clear all your blocks or not, your natural magic is still quite powerful. Magic is an ongoing process, so you don't have to get rid of it all at once, and no single witch can become entirely block-free. The good thing is that magic doesn't demand perfection. Rather, it demands uniqueness.

In a case where you can't state a specific intention because you don't know what you want, you might benefit from setting an all-purpose intention. There are two powerful all-purpose intentions to try:

"Today, the Universe bestows an unexpected gift on me."

"Today, I receive the clarity I need to know what I want."

Try the tips in this chapter to set your intentions. Keep track of results from spells and rituals. Observe patterns that show up to see if some intentions work better for you.

Remember that intention-setting is highly personal. You're likely to discover more methods that work for you as you advance in your practice. Over time, there will be more consistent results from your magical workings.

Chapter 7: Magical Knots to Know

This chapter is all about knots and the different magical knots you can tie. You will learn step-by-step instructions on how to tie several types of magical knots, such as witches' ladder, stone knot, the knot of Hercules, bowline knot, drawing knots, and so on. We will also discuss the symbolism associated with these knots.

There are several distinct types of magic knots, each with its own set of applications and backstory. The origin of the term "tying the knot" can be traced back to ancient Roman times when couples would tie a knot as part of their wedding ceremony. The Witch's Knot, also known as the Magic Knot or Witch's Charm, comprises four vesica piscis shapes linked together.

Drawing Knots and Their Significance in Magic

Knots are tied around the area where someone is experiencing pain for relief. Other magical purposes for knots include protection from witchcraft, binding a person or an object to prevent its use, and strengthening or weakening a spell.

Knots can be tied on cords, vines, twigs of trees, leather straps, pretty much anything flexible enough for you to loop around two ends together at least once. There is evidence that knots have been used in ancient times as well.

Knots are also drawn or painted on a floor or wall to represent an area of power.

Similar to how color and herbs are used in magic, knots also have their own significance:

> • A knot that is untied can be seen as ending something (i.e., breaking the spell or releasing one's self from an obligation)

> • Knots with three loops are often used for protection spells, especially if the knot is tied around something that has already been blessed

Some of the magic knots are:

> • **The Gordian Knot** – To undo a knot represents the ending of something, so it can be used to break spells or release a person from their obligation.

> • **The Shepherds Knot** – This knot is used for healing and protection when cast over a person or an object. It is also commonly seen with the clove hitch, which is said to be good

luck in Ireland, particularly if you find one on your way out of the church.

• **The Witch Knot** – This knot symbolizes the bindings of someone who has been bewitched. It is also used to bind a person or object for protection against evil forces.

Witches' Knot

The Witch's Knot, also known as the Magic Knot or Witch's Charm, comprises four vesica piscis shapes linked together.

The vesica piscis is formed by the intersection of two circles with the same radius so that the centers of each circle are on the other's perimeter. The Latin name translates as "fish bladder." The form is also known as the almond or mandorla in Italian.

The Celts and pagan cultures throughout northern Europe and pagan cultures throughout northern Europe recognized the link between this sign and birth, feminine sexuality, fertility, and the natural power of females.

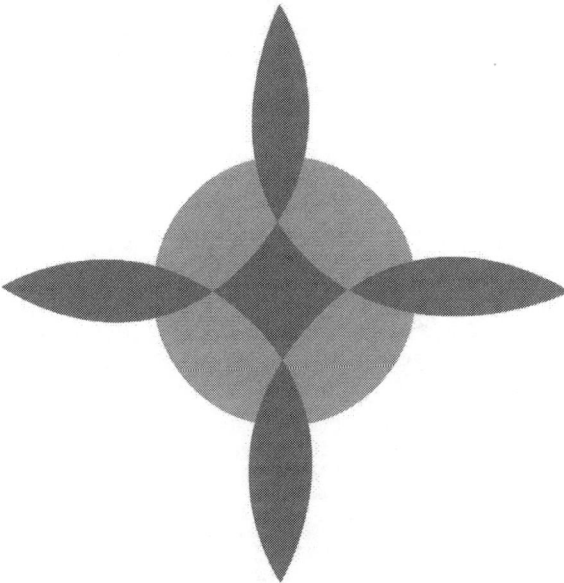

The Witch's Knot may be drawn in a single, continuous line, allowing you to draw the Witch's Knot without ever lifting your pen from the page. Therefore, it is a symbol of protection. In the past, witches used knotted ropes to 'tie up' the weather, magically bind items, and create protective rings.

Many contemporary witches have chosen this design as their preferred symbol. Consider using this chant while drawing the Witch Knot to protect yourself from any negative energy. The symbol can be drawn on your photograph or your body. When drawing the symbol, it is best to think about the positive and protective energy you wish to generate.

"By the dragon's light, on this night... I call to thee to give me your might. By the power I conjure thee, to protect all that surrounds me. As above, so below. So, mote it be!"

Gordian Knot

The Gordian Knot is tied in a complex knot, which takes a tremendously long time to untie.

After trying and failing to undo it, Alexander the Great took his sword out and cut through the knot, unraveling it, and went on to conquer Asia with ease. Legend has it that, by doing so, Alexander the Great tied together two continents.

The Gordian Knot is a metaphor for several different complex problems that can be solved easily by thinking outside the box rather than overthinking them or trying to unravel them.

There are many interpretations about what this knot actually represents and how one should go about untying it. Some say it is a metaphor of life and its complexities, whereas others believe that several knots within the larger knot need to be unraveled to untie the whole thing.

Cords Used in Magic

Cords are used for many magical purposes. They can be worn on the body to provide protection, tied into knots with specific symbolism and power attached to them, or cords can simply be an item you use in your spell casting, like knotting it around a candle during ritual work. There's no limit to what you can do with a cord, so get creative.

Cords are typically made from silk or cotton, and the color of the cords doesn't always matter. It is more important that you feel connected emotionally to the cord than its color.

Cords can be used to bind things, like your poppet or a picture of the person you're working on. You could also use cords for protection and to repel negative energy by tying knots into them. Perhaps one knot for every time someone has wronged you during the last week. You can make cords part of your altar or ritual tools, like using them to tie candles into place.

Cords can be used in everyday work, too. For instance, knot a cord around the stems of flowers before putting them in water, – and this will help keep those cuttings healthy and thriving.

A witch can use any type of string she has on hand, including thread, yarn, twine, and ribbons. Any length and material will do. Some witches keep a specific stash or use any old bit they come across. However, it is preferable to cleanse it first to ensure it does not include energies that might disrupt the spell.

Witches may choose a color corresponding to the purpose of their practice. Usually, the cords will have nine knots on them. According to symbolism, or when the witch wants to denote a quantity (less, small, or more), the number of knots will vary. At other times, a knot will be tied for every chant for meditation purposes.

Knots are often used for binding spells. This spell can be cast on a person, a piece of clothing, or even a hair braid. However, these spells are often used on phenomena rather than on people (e.g., the weather).

Sometimes, the knot will act as a container of magic. Hence, when a knot is released, the accompanying magic is also released.

The Witches' Ladder

A witches' ladder is a cord with either 3, 9, 13, or even 40 knots, with magical charms tied in for specific spell effects.

You may tie in different charms for different effects.

For example, to bring good luck, tie in a four-leaf clover charm, and a coin for wealth charms, and so on. This is one of the most common knots used within magical practice today.

Instructions:

1. Decide the intent of the Witches' Ladder - health, prosperity, or general well-being. You can also go for several benefits combined, such as health and prosperity.

2. Collect a set of either 3, 9, or 13 charms to begin with.

3. Customize the charms specifically for the benefit you are seeking. For example, select a chicken's feather for protection, a wishbone for luck, a piece of driftwood for balance, etc.

4. Tie the charms into one end of your cord or yarn with an overhand knot. Leave some space between each charm if you wish to place them in order of importance instead.

5. Using either scissors or thread clippers, cut off any excess string from both ends.

6. Make a loop at one end so that you can hang up your charm.

7. Bless each charm for the benefit you seek from it while tying it into the cord.

8. As you tie each knot, chant a spell, or wish to be granted.

9. Hang your Witches' Ladder charm in an area where its effects will be most beneficial for you, preferably somewhere you see it every day.

Always keep in mind that the Witches' Ladder's magic is only as strong as your belief and conviction. So, you must truly believe in the power of knots and magic charms.

The Square Knot

The Square Knot is a knot with two overhand knots and has been used for centuries in sailing to secure ropes.

It is one of the most important and widely used basic knots, mainly due to its simplicity. It is also known as the Reef Knot or Granny Knot since it tends to jam when tied loosely, making it all too easy to untie.

The first principle of the square knot is that it should never be used to join two separate ropes. A bend is created when you do this; d misusing the square knot as a bend may result in serious problems or total failure of your spell.

This knot should be used when you want wounds to heal quickly or enter into a short-term partnership. Untie this knot to symbolize an untrustworthy relationship, as it is connected to untrustworthy connections since it unties readily. It is a good idea to incorporate it in a spell for contracts you're not too sure about.

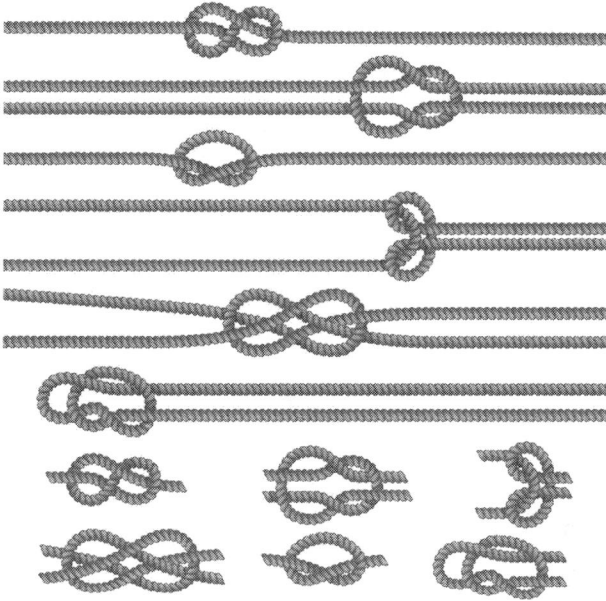

Instructions:

1. Take the two ends of the rope, and wrap them around each other twice

2. Now, simply put the right side rope over the left side rope

3. Now, pull all 4 pieces of rope away from each other to tighten the knot.

A few more ways of tying the square knot are illustrated above.

Bowline Knot

The witch's bowline is a knot that may be used to assist someone or get them out of a bind, like the actual knot. It is beneficial for individuals who have fallen down holes or over cliffs due to an accident. It can also help someone deal with drifting, much like the actual knot is used on ships.

When a witch needs to cease or slow someone down, they may whip out a tied bowline knot and untie it while incanting or tie it to the individual or problem in question. Bowlines can also be made considerably more useful when performed one-handed and with either hand. You may keep bowlines tied with the right hand for charms and rescues, while those tied with the left hand are reserved for taking people back.

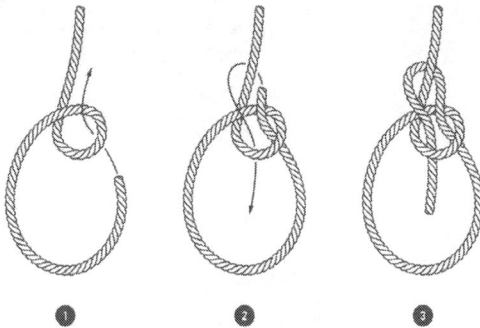

BOWLINE KNOT

Instructions:

1. Make a small loop towards the end of the cord.

2. Now, draw the smaller edge from this loop, around the cord, and back down from the small loop.

The Bottle Sling

When used in combination with a bound poppet, the sling knot helps speed up and ease recovery for individuals with musculoskeletal problems or fractured bones.

They are also used like amulets to cool anger and passion, as well as other circumstances.

JUG KNOT

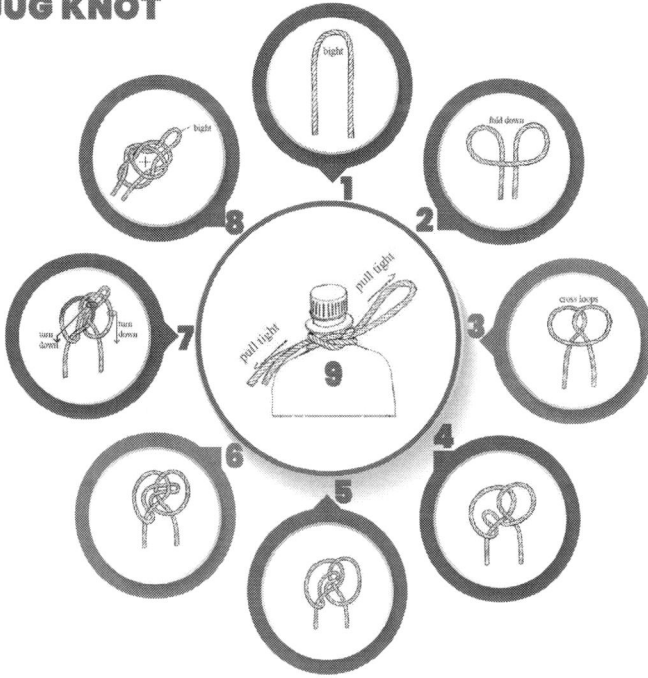

There's the concept of bottling a storm. You'll require a bottle with a cork and your twine, rope, or whatever you're using to form the sling. Once you know that a storm is coming, create a sling and place it around a bottle, slightly loose. Whistle in the storm air in deep breaths and blow it into the bottle. Now, cork the bottle up quickly and store the bottle. Open the bottle when in need of rain. It is important to ensure you only have one bottled storm at a time.

Knots Used in Amulets

Amulets are used as charms to provide protection from negative energies and entities. In some cases, amulets are also created for healing purposes or even to create a particular state of mind.

There are magical knots that can be used with amulets for different purposes.

Specific types of knot magic include Celtic Knots, Chinese Knots, and Hermetic knots, among others. The following sections discuss the uses of these knots in amulets and their history.

Celtic Knot Amulet

The Celtic knot is very common in history and can be found in architecture, art, jewelry, and even tattoos.

This knot is often associated with the concept of infinity or reincarnation because it cannot be undone without cutting one strand from the whole, which is impossible. Furthermore, when looking at a Celtic Knot amulet sideways, they create an M shape that symbolizes protection, among other things.

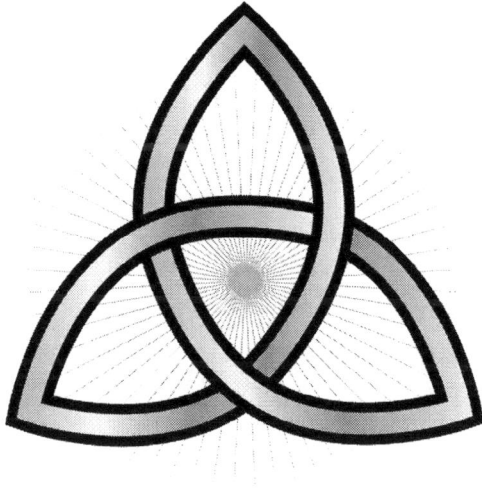

Celtic Knots were believed to confer magical powers, such as protection and healing. They also had divinatory properties where the Celtic knots meanings could only be viewed from a certain perspective, usually sideways.

Chinese Knot Amulet

The Chinese knot is a very common amulet that uses knots of different kinds to create shapes and amulets. Depending on the shape, they have different meanings and powers.

Chinese Knot Amulets were also used as a protective amulet to ward off negative energies and entities, especially those that had to do with floods or water accidents. They can be worn around the neck for this purpose but are usually found in homes, too.

https://pixabay.com/zh/photos/tea-box-with-the-wish-to-3170045/

Magical knots are an important part of our culture and folklore, but they're also practical tools. Knowing how to tie these knots will come in handy whether you need to tie something down or get out of a tight situation. This chapter covers step-by-step instructions for tying several types of magical knots like the witches' ladder, stone knot, the knot of Hercules, bowline knot, drawing knots, and more. It also includes symbolism about some famous knots, such as the Witch's Knot and Gordian Knot. Learning knots is the easier part, but it is essential to have faith in your practice when using the techniques, and you understand the importance and power of learning how to make knots.

Chapter 8: The Standard Knit Spell

Knot spells are all about the energy you reflect and your intentions as you prepare your spells. These spells are incredibly versatile and can be used for a wide array of purposes. You may be surprised to learn that you can cast an incredibly powerful spell with just about anything that allows you to tie it into a knot. These knots can be as simple as tying a bow or as complex and intricate as a macrame plant hanger. There is no limit to what you can do with knot spells. The most important thing is that you aim for things that genuinely resonate with you because your intentions are the driving force behind the spell. If you don't believe or want it with every fiber of your being, the chances are that the spell will not work.

Almost every spell can be conducted using a knot, and you can use this technique or form of magic to attract wealth and abundance, protection, to make curses, healing spells, binding spells, luck, and prosperity spells. The use of knots is very common in the world of witchcraft, which shows just how effective or significant knot rituals are. If you've been reading into witchcraft and magic, then you probably think of cord-cutting spells when you first hear the words "knot" or "cord."

You can think of cord-cutting as a healing method or technique. It offers a way to disengage from unhealthy and emotionally draining circumstances that eat up mental energy. Cord-cutting doesn't aim to eliminate healthy relationships in your life. Instead, it aids you in getting rid of the emotional blocks that limit your mindset and overall well-being. When done correctly, you can speed up the healing process and remove all relational attachment cords, and this helps your relationships grow into nurturing bonds or more evolved connections. You may even find yourself outgrowing some relationships altogether by cord-cutting. It is not done to hurt you or make you lose people in your life, but it is to help you reach a higher vibrational, mental, emotional, and spiritual state. You learn to get rid of things and people that don't serve you and bind you to a lower vibrational state. Cutting cords can help you become more enlightened and a lot wiser. One Buddhist teaching even explains that attachment is the core reason behind our suffering. So, think of cord-cutting as a technique that frees your soul from situations and people that don't serve your best interest. It is a way to break free from the anchor that chains you to lower vibrational states and paves the way to a more self-actualized journey. Performing this spell requires you to physically tie a knot and break it to signify the release of unhelpful patterns. Interestingly, a knot spell is broken if the cord is broken.

This chapter teaches all about knot spells. You will understand how a simple knot magic spell looks and why this process is quite important, as well as grasp how the process works from start to finish. Upon reading this chapter, you will find helpful chants and realize that there is much more to knot magic spells than cutting bonds or leaving things behind. You will learn about the order these knots need to be untied and how to cancel a spell if you've changed your mind about the things you want (or don't want) in life.

Energy Cords: Can We See Them?

Our mind's eye is capable of seeing and feeling energy cords and surges around us. Our mind's eye is the area in our brains responsible for recollecting memories and creating vivid images. The form in which these cords appear to us is purely symbolic. How we see these cords depends on the relationship's emotional dynamics. There is no one way to define energy cords, how they appear, and the types of emotions they stir up. Energy or relational cords can feel like anything. They can feel like streams of joy and delight or like barbed wires. Just like our mind visualizes these cords, it can imagine an appropriate tool to chop them off. Typically, this is the foundation of cord-cutting rituals since the energy that binds us to other people and things in life is quite powerful, then it surely plays a great role in knot spells.

There is much variation as to what these cords are attached to. Though, typically, chakras play a significant role in this attachment. Chakras are our energy centers. For instance, healthy, loving, and positive relationships are connected to the heart chakra. Meanwhile, a relationship where you feel controlled, suppressed, or denied the ability to express yourself might be felt at the throat chakra. Wherever these cords are connected, they can take a tremendous toll on your body and physical well-being.

You must have a "will" mindset to conduct your spell successfully. "Will" is your driving force and your belief that you are working toward some form of change. Energy cords exist at the subconscious and unconscious levels and can greatly affect your life. By allowing your subconscious mind to believe that you can fuel these desires, you are reinforcing the energy cords that lie between you and the things you want. So, believing in your intentions is the most important part of the spell.

Cords of Attachment

Cords of attachment are the cords that hold unhealthy or problematic relationships. As we mentioned above, these cords can affect people differently. They can impact us on different levels and persist for varying timeframes. Some people suffer from unhelpful cords of attachment for a lifetime. Let's say you have an energy cord with a highly controlling individual. If they want to exert their control over you, it will undeniably feel incredibly and consciously intrusive. However, cords of attachment found within healthy or pure relationships, such as we have with our pets, affect us on a more subconscious level. According to professional intuitive healers, cords of attachment form whenever an unfulfilled need or desire is found between you and another person. If either of your efforts is not reciprocated, or if one person feels unequal to the other, this creates an intrusive presence, leading to a lower vibration. Whenever you struggle with lower vibrations, your energy field becomes blocked and triggers negative, intrusive thoughts. It may feel like these relationships are constantly sustained by the need for control, power, or suppression, as well as feelings of anxiety or fear. These are precisely the types of relationships that require cord-cutting.

Similarly, a cord of attachment that exists between you and something you desire can become negative. Suppose you've been feeling under the weather or have been obsessing over this desire for a while. In that case, best that you release this negativity before partaking in knot magic because some rituals require you to burn or bury your knots after conducting the spell, signifying release.

Knot Spell

Knot spells are quite easy and can be used for many purposes. They are not explicitly designed to help you get rid of toxic individuals or unhealthy relationships. Knot spells or rituals can be used to prevent yourself or others from experiencing harm, aid in healing painful physical sensations, avoid nightmares, help with healing headaches, guide you toward releasing feelings of anger or hatred, and even aid in protecting yourself or your home. You can perform almost any type of spell using a knot. As mentioned, the best thing about knot spells is that they are fueled by intention and our tendency to believe that we will acquire whatever it is that we're working towards and aiming for.

https://unsplash.com/photos/brown-rope-on-blue-wooden-table-9ycXTLGNMro

You can think of knot spells as a means of binding the things you wish for. You are, literally and metaphorically, tying up your intentions into a knot to bind them into your life. This knot serves as an anchor point to the things you want in life. You can perform any spell using a knot and manifest anything you want. Similarly, you can use any knot to cast a spell. You don't need to be a certified witch or a crochet master to ensure that your spell is effective. If you prefer, you can make a spell from only one knot, anytime and anywhere you desire. The trick is to do whatever makes the most sense to you, and it resonates best with your intentions.

You don't need to shop around town to gather 50 ingredients to throw your spell together. To create a successful spell, you don't need a cauldron, sage, incense, crystals, essential, or salt. Perhaps, this is what makes knot spells so special. By limiting the number and types of materials, you need to use and the number of steps to conduct it, you can guarantee that your focus and efforts are directed toward the right purpose, which is why you are conducting the spell.

All you need to do is acquire natural material, such as rope, yarn, cord, wires, vines, scarves, or anything you can tie into a knot. Make sure that you aren't using a synthetic material, as these are free of magical charge, and use each cord only once. Using it several times means that you will be blending several intentions, and this isn't a good idea as it can pollute your magic and weaken it.

The first step to conducting knot magic is finding out what you want to do exactly. Do you want to attract a healthy relationship? Do you want to get your dream job? Do you desire protection? Are you using knot magic to heal a certain ailment? When you get a clear idea of your intentions, you need to identify the approach you will be using to conduct your spell.

When preparing for a knot ritual, you must take one of two approaches, either reactive or proactive. The proactive approach requires you to be prepared long before you conduct your ritual, meaning that you need to prepare for your spell ahead of time to improve a specific circumstance or avoid troubles. For instance, long ago, witches used to place the winds into knots as per the request of sailors to avoid calamities or getting stuck into a dead calm. If they got stuck, they used to untie one of the knots to release the wind.

Most knot spells are done proactively, meaning that people don't wait for disaster to strike, so they can work their way through it by using magic. Instead, they use knot spells beforehand to avoid issues and pitfalls or at least be prepared to navigate through rapid waters.

Steps to Take

As we mentioned above, your intention and ability to believe in whatever you are manifesting are the only way you'll get your spell to work. You need to practice a technique known as "panic breathing" to help guide you through the process. This is a method that many yoga practitioners are aware of and use actively. To conduct this exercise, you need to breathe in deeply so your stomach expands. Make sure to put all your lung's capacity to use. While doing so, imagine if you were pulling up as much energy as you could from the earth beneath you. This breathing technique allows you to move energy, which, as we explained, plays a significant role in manifestation, knot spells, and cord-cutting techniques. Envision your breath as if it were a blue-green-colored mist that transports your intentions and beliefs into the knot.

1. Think deeply about what you need. Why did you think about conducting this spell in the first place?

2. Be clear about the intentions you set. Take the time to repeat to yourself positive, future-oriented statements relevant to your intentions. This will help you reinforce your belief in this spell and its tendency to work.

3. Start tying the knot while focusing on your intention:

As we explained, the number of cords and knots you make should be relevant to your intention and feel natural to you. Let's say you want to manifest happiness, abundance, and peace. Therefore, to conduct your knot spell, you will have three strings, and each is 36 inches long. Combine your knots together and tie them in the following order: (left to right) 1-6-4-7-3-8-5-9-2. While knotting the cords, you need to focus on your intentions (try not to tighten the knots just yet). It is beneficial to repeat a mantra, such as:

By knot of one, this spell has begun

By knot of two, my words are true

By knot of three, it comes to be

By knot of four, this power is stored

By knot of five, the spell is alive

By knot of six, the spell is fixed

By knot of seven, the answer is given

By knot of eight, I meld with fate

By knot of nine, the thing is mine!

There are several similar mantras that people use during knot spells. You can search for them and use the one you resonate with the most. You can also come up with your own chant or change the number of your knots if these examples don't resonate with you (please refer to chapter 5 on numerology to make sure you get it right). Magic and spells are supposed to be about you, which is why you can tweak them for your comfort.

4. Engage in the panic breathing technique that we explained above.

5. Keep your desires and intentions fixed deeply in your head. Envision them as if they were your reality, even if you were only able to do so for no more than a second or two. At this moment, you need to blow your will (remember the green-blue-colored mist?) into the knot(s) and proceed to tighten them.

6. After you have finished, take the time to ground yourself.

Things to Look Out For

As you now know, a spell goes in vain once a knot is untied. Your knot is a physical symbol of your intentions and spell, and if it breaks, so does your spell. However, this isn't always a disadvantage, as it makes it easy for you to undo a spell whenever necessary. Merely undo the knots if your intention doesn't resonate with you anymore.

Everything that surrounds us is a form of energy. Our friends, family, pets, work, and home are all energy. Each of these carries a different form or essence of energy, which, in turn, forms these cords and shapes how we respond to them. Knot spells are all about intention and, therefore, have to do with energy, too. Our intentions fuel our sub-conscience, so by staying positive and truly believing in the power we hold to achieve what we want or obtain the things we desire, we reinforce a positive connection with these things. Being positive raises our overall vibrations, which increases the chances that the spell might work.

Chapter 9: Knot Spells for Love and Protection

This chapter focuses on knot spells for love and protection. It explains different knot spells, instructions on how to conduct them, and recommended times to do the spell. Some of the common knots covered in this chapter include love binding, lover's knot, cutting the cord, home protection, and more. When you decide to practice spells, make sure you do not infringe on someone's fights or cause harm with binding spells since they can backfire.

Types of Magic

You can perform different types of magic with a cord, string, knotted ribbon, or anything symbolic. If you want to perform magic, make sure you use something symbolic like a simple knot. Cord or knot magic has been used to get rid of an illness or other unwanted things since time immemorial. When you tie a knot, it represents the problem you want to cast away. The principle behind this spell is that all your challenges will be bound to the cord and leave you a free person.

Knot Magic Spell to Heal Sickness

You can use this spell to heal, and you will need a string that is 8 inches long. On the string, mark it six times to give you seven equal parts. The next step is to recite each statement below six times and tie a knot until you get six knots.

"Disease, no one asks your stay, it is time for you to go, with these knots, I ask you to go, I weave with these words."

When you finish, place the string in a container with salt and seal it. Bury the rope in salt to symbolize the way you bury your sickness in the earth. Use a paper with the written incarnation on top to make a seal of the container. Properly dispose of the container to mark the end of your ritual. You can do this by burying the container or throwing it in running water.

Knot Spell to Clear Evil Curse

You can utilize the knot spell to remove an evil curse when you feel that someone does not like you. Someone may direct negativity toward you to make you sick or experience other bad things simply because of hatred. The energy can cause issues like disappointments and bad luck in life. So, when you are in a predicament like this, cast a spell to clear you of the negativity.

You need to confess your situation and say positive words to sweep away negativity from your life. You can also use a spell to return the bad luck or misfortune to the sender. You need a bottle and a string to perform this spell, and all you need to do is tie a knot on the string and place it in your bottle. Then, bury the bottle with the contents in the earth.

After three days, dig up the bottle, place it on the ground, and recite the following statements.

"A curse on me buried deep, to make me sick, you damn it creep. I place a knot on this string, so your work is in vain."

The next step is to break the bottle and remove the string carefully to undo the curse. Untie the knot and dispose of the broken bottle pieces safely. Take the cord and burn it and blow the remaining ashes in the wind. This spell can guide you perfectly, especially if you include meditation. The string will carry away the curse. You may need a love drawing mojo like the following to carry out this spell.

Get Well Mojo and Love-Drawing Mojo

The Spell for Cutting the Cord When you're physically, spiritually, and emotionally connected with someone, you form a bond that resembles a crimson thread and becomes bound. When a relationship abruptly ends, however, it is extremely difficult for either of you to move on since you are still connected in some way. If your relationship has irreversibly broken down, you must use the Cutting Cord Spell to sever any remaining links and let each of you move on.

To perform this spell, you need a length of red cord, a picture of your ex-lover or friend, a pair of scissors, and two candles. Before starting the ritual, cleanse yourself and cast a magical circle where you set out the materials. Write your name on the first candle and the other person's name on the second candle. Use anointing oil to charge the candles starting from the center, moving outward, so the energy will go out. You must see the other person's name on the candle while anointing it.

Hold the first candle in your hand over the altar, visualizing it is charged with the energy you will use to do your bidding. Present your candle to the altar and make the following: mention that you acknowledge the goddess who gave substance and form to our spirits, and you are also giving form and substance to the candle. Insert the other party's name and state that the candle is made of wick and wax, so is our flesh and body.

Repeat the same process to the second candle and sit in a meditation position. Consider all of the happiness that the other person has brought into your life and recall the greatest occasions. Consider the strong crimson rope that binds your hearts together. Each string end should be tied to a candle to symbolize the spirit joining you. Say something to the goddess while placing the photo in the center of the string; "As the spirit links people together, these two forms also do the same below, above, and within."

Sit in a meditation position and think of all the reasons you want to terminate the ties with the other person you have known for a long time. Consider all of the variables that went into making this decision, as well as your worries and doubts. You should know that the goddess only wants the best for you. Visualize yourself telling your ex-partner that it is over between you both –and you are moving on. Consider moving away from yourself and never looking back.

Cut the cord that has been binding you and the image you placed between the candles and say to the goddess that you are taking this action by your free will. State that you do not intend to harm anyone from the action you are about to take. Say that you are severing the cord between you and the other person. You must also state that you cherish the journey you have walked together, but you are now taking different paths, although you wish to reach the same destination.

You must release another person's name from any ties with you and give you freedom. Place the candle with half the picture and half the cord in a heatproof bowl. Put some goodwill incense and mentholated spirit and light them. As the smoke rises, imagine that all your ties to the other person are dissolving as well. If you prefer to do so, you can light your candle on the altar. Clean the circle and bury everything once the ceremony is over. However, you must not bury your candle since you leave it burning to its end.

Knot Magick (Binding) Spells

Knot or cord magic is potent for witchcraft and is also known as binding. Binding is a spell that attaches one individual or energy to the other. However, this type of spell can be dangerous, especially if practiced by a novice. Therefore, you must enlist the services of a professional if you want to undertake this type of spell to avoid causing harm.

To perform this spell, you must buy appropriate focus bead and color, depending on what you want to achieve. You can use different numbers to tie the knots on your cord to perform your desired spellwork. Remember, you can use the same cord to perform various spells. All you need to do is choose the appropriate string that suits the ritual you want to perform. It is a good idea to consult a professional magician first before you obtain the required materials.

Commitment Spells

Are you wondering how you can make your partner committed to you? You can perform a commitment spell if you want to improve your relationship or get your lost lover back. If the ritual is done correctly, this spell will never backfire. To perform this spell, you need specific ingredients that include a red ribbon, a piece of paper, a red and white candle, a black marker, a picture of your lover, and a black cloth.

You begin the session by writing your lover's name thrice on the piece of paper using a black marker. Place a lit red candle on the right side and another white one on the left. Place the paper between the two burning candles and place the picture of your estranged lover on the paper. Wrap the items using a clean black cloth and use a red ribbon to tie the top of the black cloth. Lift the black bag so that its bottom is above the red candle.

Ask God to hear your prayers and bring back your lover while holding the black bag of contents. Repeat the process using the white candle and bury the bag in the soil to seal the spell. You should see the results of this spell in a short period, and it works best at night when there is a full moon. Clear any worries from your mind when performing the spell since they can affect your spell.

Marriage Spells

If you need to improve your marital life, consider marriage spells since they can make a significant difference. Marriage spells consist of commitment spells, and they can guarantee lasting effects in your love life. If you want to make your spouse loyal to you, this spell can be your perfect choice. A red silk cord is the only ingredient you need. Put the cord under your pillow when bedtime arrives, and it must remain in the same position until the time you sleep.

You must wait for your partner to sleep deeply, then pull out your cord and tie seven knots on it. You must keep the cord in a safe and private area when no one can access it. As long as all the knots are not loosened, you will enjoy loyalty from your partner. Don't discuss the spell casting act with anyone since the power will decrease if it is revealed

Your energy is the primary key to the success of your spell. If you invest in positive energy, you will reap positive results. You must connect with the power of nature and the universe if you want to succeed in your love spell. Love can attract love, especially if you focus on good things that can appeal to the emotional interests of other people.

When you cast your spells at home or decide to get help from a professional, there are various things to do to achieve your goals. It is essential to focus your attitude and thoughts – and believe that it will happen. In other words, you must have faith, confidence, and patience in your spell. Remember, some love spells may take longer, so do not lose hope. When negativity creeps into your mind, turn it into positivity. As long as there is a positive environment surrounding you, love will visit you.

Chapter 10: Knot Spells for Abundance and Luck

As you know, you can use knot spells to manifest just about anything you want, making knot magic the perfect tool for manifesting luck and abundance. Luck and abundance are among the two most important things in life, and they are two things everyone in the world wishes they possessed. Being lucky is a gift that no wise person would ever trade for the world. Think about the countless individuals who have made it to the top through sheer luck. When observing the statistics for the most influential and successful people globally, you can't help but think that they are simply the luckiest people on Earth.

Hard work is not enough if you want to receive tenure at the highest departments. Millions of people work tirelessly, day and night, dedicate their lives to their careers, work in progress, always gather new information and resources, and put so much effort into networking, yet they don't amount to much. On the other hand, other people can do as little as post a video on a social media platform, it goes viral, and they have several contracts lined up. Think about all the talents that have become world-famous merely because they were lucky enough. For instance, John Crosby, a Hollywood manager, was at a bank at the same time as Charlize Theron, who was arguing with a bank teller. After he witnessed the entire argument, he decided to sign her for her first role. Mel Gibson, who got into a fight the night before he promised to drop his friend off at an audition, was told by the director to come back because the movie "needs freaks." After his face had healed, Gibson starred in Mad Max. Pamela Anderson was immediately signed as a model after her face was shown on a football game's big screen.

What we're saying is that even if you work very hard, you are still unlikely to get anywhere or achieve great things unless you're at least somewhat lucky. We are always very quick to point out disadvantages or things that aren't going our way, and this is why we overlook the role that luck plays in our lives. We also overestimate our abilities. While our potential has a lot to do with luck and our ability to succeed in the path that luck offers, we are not entirely responsible for these successes. Without our intuition, we wouldn't be able to recognize the opportunities that luck presents to us and act on them.

Abundance is also incredibly essential, especially in the fast-paced world in which we live. While being financially abundant is a top priority, there is so much more abundance than just your financial status. Many people experience romantic abundance, relational (friendships and professional relationships) abundance, abundance in energy, abundance in resources, and even abundance in fun. Abundance comes in many shapes and forms. So, being an abundant individual and experiencing abundance in several areas of life is one of the best gifts the universe can ever grant you. Besides being lucky, you need to be prosperous in several areas of life to ensure that you have the resources to get where you need to be in life. Many people have sufficient financial resources but lack the emotional and social abundance needed to maintain healthy relationships and partake in networking activities.

Therefore, knot spells offer an invaluable gift. They offer you the chance to create an abundant life for yourself and attract luck and good fortune. These qualities make up the recipe for a successful, enjoyable, and rewarding life. These are all the things you need to pave your path to affluence, influence, power, respect, and happiness. There's a very famous Arabic saying that translates to "one carat of luck is much better than an acre of cleverness." It means that even if you're the cleverest person on earth, you're still not going to amount to much unless luck is involved. This chapter offers you numerous knot spells dedicated to helping you attract anything related to prosperity, abundance, getting a dream job, luck, and attracting money.

Knot Spell for Prosperity, Abundance, Getting a Dream Job, Luck and Attracting Money

Ingredients:

- 3 cords, 9 inches each
- Agate stone
- Tiger's eye stone
- Orange ribbon
- A candle (preferably green)
- Pins with green heads
- Incense

- Sage

- Holy water (optional)

- Herbs: Myrrh, basil, cinnamon, frankincense, high John the conqueror, patchouli, skullcaps, vanilla, garlic, peppermint, rosemary, passionflower, roses, thyme, nettle, chamomile, cloves, dill, jasmine, perforate St John's Wort, catnip, vervain, valerian, eyebright, rue, and cayenne.

Procedure:

Gather the three 9-inch cords. Collect them together and tie them into three knots. The number three is a very significant divine number in the world of witchcraft. With each knot sequence you make, you're going to repeat three words out loud. These three words should be related to your intention. In your case, you can say the words success, reward, and abundance. As you tie the first knot, say the word success. Say the word reward as you tie your second knot and the word abundance with your third knot. Repeat this process three times, tying each knot on top of its previous corresponding knot. You need to focus on your intention with each knot you make. Manifest it and breathe it into the loop. Think about your promotion or the job offer of your dreams as you tie each knot.

Look up prosperity and wealth chants to whisper into your cord as you knot it. However, the three main words should be enough.

When you're done, proceed to tie all these knots together multiple times to make one large knot. Don't forget the three words mentioned earlier. When you have turned your cords into one large knot, gather your crystals. We mentioned previously that the best thing about knot spells is they don't require numerous materials and much effort, so crystals aren't a vital part of the process. However, stones are used purely to enhance the overall energy and promote power. Agate stones are generally associated with wealth, abundance, and luck. Tiger's eyes are good for prosperity, wealth, love, and abundance. You need an orange ribbon as it symbolizes abundance and prosperity. If you prefer, you can use a green ribbon, which is linked to money. Either way, you are using a green candle (it doesn't have to be) and pins with green heads.

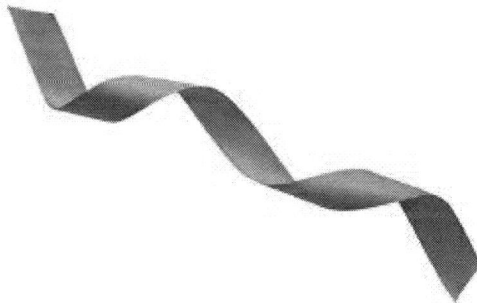

Use the orange ribbon to wrap the knot entirely. Stick a few pins into the ribbon and through the knot to help hold it together. (It also symbolically pierces through the knot, allowing luck to flow out and onto you.) Take your candle and take out its wick. Insert the wick into the ribbon and the knot creating a candle to use during the ritual. Place the candle or wax inside a heat-resistant glass. Place it in boiling water to liquefy it. At this point, you need to add an herbal mixture, which we will discuss shortly, and then place the wick and the ribbon-wrapped knot into the melted wax. Make sure that the wick is held upward. Leave the wax to dry.

Herbal Mixture

Light some incense and prepare your space to clear it of bad energy you don't want around. Charge and bless your space and all your instruments using burning sage. If you prefer, you can use holy water to keep your working space extra blessed.

https://unsplash.com/photos/lighted-incense-12PwFpWZZ0

It doesn't matter which type of mixture or herbs you use, as long as it resonates with your intentions and makes sense to you. However, we'll provide an example of a very powerful, comprehensive herbal mixture to aid abundance and luck.

You need to know that this mixture doesn't follow standard measurements or a specific recipe. Don't overthink the process, and just trust your intuition. Go with your gut feeling and what it is telling you at the time. In a pot, bowl, or cauldron, drop your myrrh. This herb serves well for abundance, concentration, honor, success, wealth, and prosperity. Then, insert your basil. Basil is the go-to herb for anything related to money, prosperity, and business. Basil is also great for promoting assertiveness, which is something that you need for your career. It also helps improve focus, attentiveness, and concentration and is great for money and confidence. You can always use it for these purposes when necessary. Sage, who you will also add, is also good for business, money, prosperity, concentration, focus, and general wealth.

Add in your cinnamon, which is great for business, concentration, and focus. It also helps generally alleviate different aspects of life. Cinnamon helps focus on self-development and enables you to stay successful at your job, make money, and grow your wealth. Drop in your frankincense, which you should have already burnt at the start. High John the Conqueror is perfect for anything that has to do with business goals. It helps focus on goals, money, and prosperity and is also associated with skills, success, and wealth. *High John the Conqueror is a power herb.*

Patchouli is also a go-to for money, business, luck, prosperity, skillset, success, and wealth. You also need to add skullcaps, which aids concentration and focus for business, promotion, and getting jobs. Vanilla is also great for concentration, focus, and success. Take a vanilla bean and snap a part of it off and drop it into your bowl.

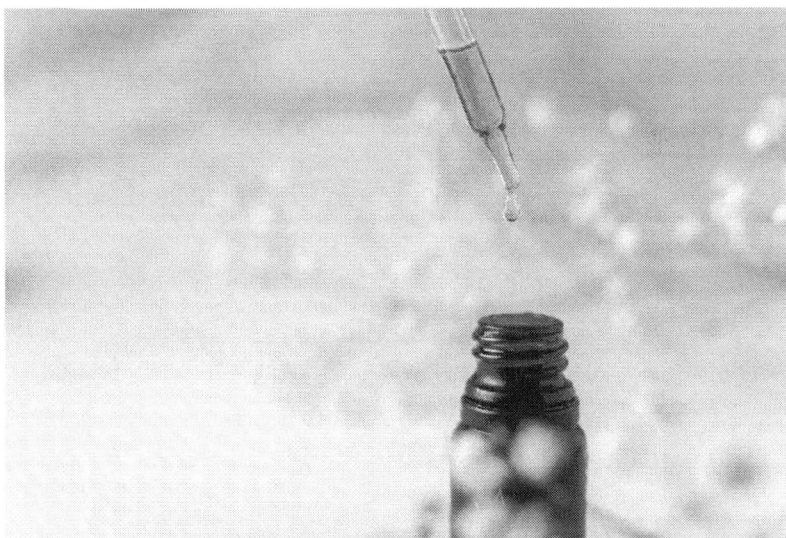

Add garlic to boost your concentration and focus and lavender to help achieve peace, comfort, and relaxation. Lavender generally helps

with everything and increases concentration, focus, determination, going after goals, luck, and manifestation. We are actively manifesting everything we desire throughout the process. Our thoughts shape our reality, and they are spells that are cast wisely. A positive mindset attracts positivity, while a negative state of mind attracts negativity.

Add peppermint into the mixture to keep refining your concentration, focus, and skills. Also, add rosemary, which is good for confidence, concentration, focus, determination, and general luck. If you struggle with a lack of confidence, you need to use extra rosemary, as confidence ensures success. You also need a passionflower for an additional confidence boost.

Roses are also great at boosting confidence, luck, and manifestation. You need to picture yourself receiving your dream job offer. This is what your spell is for exactly. You need to visualize your intentions to shift your energy since knot spells are all about intentions.

Use thyme and nettle to increase your luck, confidence, focus, and promote the abundance of money. Use chamomile, a go-to herb, to aid with luck, determination, manifestation, money, prosperity, and wealth. Chamomile is the ideal ingredient for anything related to money. Use cloves to aid with luck, prosperity, success, and wealth. You may be surprised to learn that cloves also serve as anesthetics. For instance, if you have a toothache, putting a clove on the painful area can alleviate the symptoms.

Throw in some dill and jasmine for money, luck, prosperity, and wealth, and some perforate St John's Wort to serve the same purpose. Use some catnip, which serves as an attractor. Catnip can be used in any mixture created to serve any type of intent because catnip acts as an attractor in all cases. All you need to do is focus on what you're using the catnip for as you drop it into your mixture. Vervain aids with money, prosperity, success, and wealth. Valerian is also great for the money, while eyebright is excellent for honing your skills. Rue is excellent for attracting luck and helping us develop the mental power we need to find success in life.

Finally, insert your pièce de résistance: Cayenne. Always add cayenne to any herbal mixture you create, as it acts as a catalyst and helps speed up the manifestation process. However, make sure you don't touch your eyes or skin so you don't burn or hurt yourself. After you've added all your ingredients into a bowl, mix, and grind them carefully. As you do so, make sure to focus on your intent. You also need to visualize and feel everything you want, and it helps to have incense burning in the background. When done, put your mixture into a small bottle and store it away.

If you need to create a mixture really quickly, you can use chamomile and basil for a money knot spell.

If you think about it, everything in life is founded on luck. Those who are born in countries with prosperous economies are luckier than those born in poorer countries. Individuals born into wealthy families are a lot luckier than those who have always been less fortunate. The people you meet and the connections you make are also usually linked to how lucky you are. Being at the right place, for the right reasons, at the right time is luck, and this is why using knot spells for luck and abundance can help keep us on the right track.

Conclusion

You have reached the end of the book; congratulations! If you take one thing away from this read, we hope it will be to understand how important knot magic and knot spells are for those who seek to use its power. Throughout history, cultures have used cords in most of their magical practices, and however, most have only scratched the surface of what cord magic has to offer.

The purpose of this book was not to teach you *all of the knots* and how to do them, as that would take hours upon hours. Rather, we hoped to give you a starting point as well as some very powerful spells you can use in your magical practice today. Knot magic is one of the most widely misunderstood forms of spell crafting for beginners and experienced magical users alike. If you have read the entire book from cover to cover, you are now on your way to mastering cord magic and knot spells.

If this is your first time attempting a spell from a non-traditional form of magic, then we hope you will approach it cautiously. Like anything in life, knot magic and knot spells work best if you do not abuse their power. It is easy to become lost in the possibilities of knot magic once you realize how incredibly powerful it can be. If abused, your cord may turn against you and leave you, like many other people, feeling disappointed and disillusioned with your practice.

Use your knot magic spells for good, not evil. If you are doing this for negative reasons, then your cord will turn against you.

Practice makes perfect in all things worth pursuing. It is the same with cord magic and knot spells. The more time and effort you put into them, the better they will work for you. Faith in yourself and your practice is the single most powerful thing a magician can have in their arsenal. If you believe, then you will succeed.

In this book, we discussed, in detail, the benefits of knot magic and cord spells and how to choose your fabrics. We also went into great depth about timing and numbers within your spells. Finally, we gave examples of several knots you can begin weaving into your magical practice today.

From chapter 5 onward, we explored knots, numerology, the knotwork processes, and the spells. We hope that you have learned a great deal from this book and can put it to good use in your magical practice.

The knots you studied in chapter 7 should be coupled with the spells from chapter 8 for the most powerful results. Also, check out the knots mentioned in chapters 9 and 10 for love, luck, prosperity, protection, and abundance.

We urge you to be safe, have fun, and practice knot magic responsibly. Knot magic is an ancient yet advanced form of spell crafting that will continue to grow in popularity within modern magical practices.

We hope you enjoyed reading this book and that you try some of the knots we discussed here.

Here's another book by Mari Silva that you might like

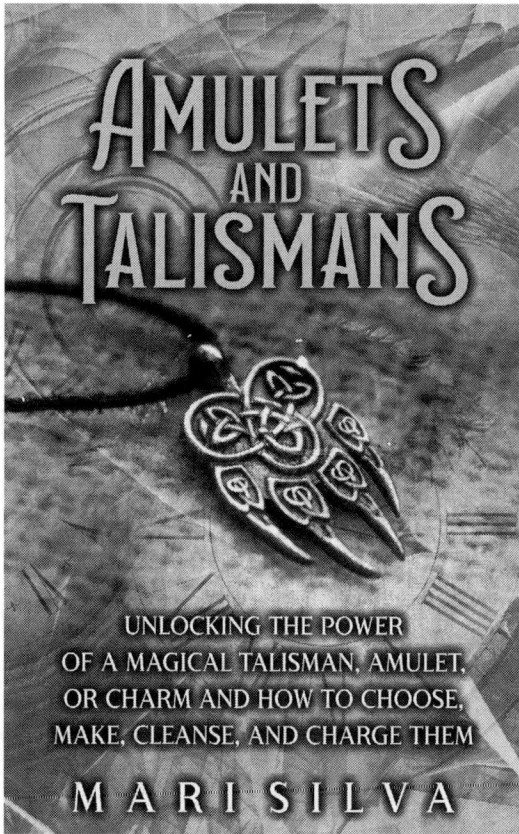

Your Free Gift (only available for a limited time)

Thanks for getting this book! If you want to learn more about various spirituality topics, then join Mari Silva's community and get a free guided meditation MP3 for awakening your third eye. This guided meditation mp3 is designed to open and strengthen ones third eye so you can experience a higher state of consciousness. Simply visit the link below the image to get started.

https://spiritualityspot.com/meditation

References

10 facts about leather you didn't know! (n.d.). Retrieved from Mahileather.com website:

https://mahileather.com/blogs/news/10-facts-about-leather-you-didn-t-know

Silvia. (n.d.). Magical Properties of metal. Retrieved from Magic-spells-and-potions.com

website: https://magic-spells-and-potions.com/magical_properties_of_metal.htm

The magic of fabrics. (2015, September 30). Retrieved from Marjolijnmakes.com website:

https://marjolijnmakes.com/writings/essays/the-magic-of-fabrics

Moon phases and simple rituals - Wicca academy. (n.d.). Retrieved from

https://wiccaacademy.com/moon-phases-and-simple-rituals

The magical planets. (2015, July 20). Retrieved from Spellsofmagic.com website:

https://www.spellsofmagic.com/coven_ritual.html?ritual=3466&coven=497

Wright, M. S. (2014, February 9). How to cast spells using magical timing based on planetary

hours. Retrieved from Exemplore website: https://exemplore.com/wicca-witchcraft/How-to-Cast-Spells-Magical-Timing-by-Planetary-Hours

Witchcraft, magick, and the planets. (2013, September 3). Retrieved from Amagickalpath.co.uk

website: https://amagickalpath.co.uk/witchcraft-magick-and-the-planets

Magickal timing: Choosing the right day of the week for your spell. (n.d.). Retrieved from

Groveandgrotto.com website:

https://www.groveandgrotto.com/blogs/articles/35309377-magical-timing-choosing-the-right-day-of-the-week-for-your-spell

Magic. (2019, April 17). Timing your magic – which moon phase to cast a spell - witchcraft, pagan, occult, and magic. Retrieved from Witcheslore.com website:

https://witcheslore.com/bookofshadows/rituals-spell-casting/time-for-magic-which-moon-phase-to-cast-a-spell/32795

Miracles, S. M. (2019, May 28). How to use the phases of the Moon for magic & spellcasting.

Retrieved from Numerologist.com website:

https://numerologist.com/numerology/moon-phases-and-magic

A sea witch's knots 101 - the bowline. (n.d.). Tumblr.Com. Retrieved from

https://skinlesswitch.tumblr.com/post/185006135973/a-sea-witchs-knots-101-the-bowline

A sea witch's knots 101 - the square knot. (n.d.). Tumblr.Com. Retrieved from

https://skinlesswitch.tumblr.com/post/184983543308/a-sea-witchs-knots-101-the-square-knot

Abloy, A. (n.d.). Magical knots. Historicallocks.Com. Retrieved from https://www.historicallocks.com/en/site/h/locks-and-magic/taboos-and-magical-knots/magical-knots

Bear, S. L. (n.d.). 11 unusual ways to use cords & knots in your magic - the traveling witch.

Thetravelingwitch.Com. Retrieved from https://thetravelingwitch.com/blog/2018/8/26/11-unusual-ways-to-use-cords-knots-in-your-magic

Definition of GORDIAN KNOT. (n.d.). Merriam-Webster.Com. Retrieved from https://www.merriam-webster.com/dictionary/Gordian%20knot

Friend, W. (n.d.). Wiccan Friend. Wordpress.Com. Retrieved from https://wiccanfriend.wordpress.com/tag/gordian-knot

A witch's guide to cord-cutting, the simple ritual to get over your ex. (n.d.). Retrieved from Vice.com website: https://www.vice.com/en/article/mbz3na/how-to-do-cord-cutting-ritual-witch-spell-breakup

Cutting energy cords for personal growth - insight timer blog. (2019, September 23). Retrieved

from Insighttimer.com website: https://insighttimer.com/blog/cutting-energy-cords

Hart, A. (n.d.). How to work knot spells: The most underrated quick magic - the traveling witch.

Retrieved from Thetravelingwitch.com website https://thetravelingwitch.com/blog/2016/12/21/knot-spells

Moonwater. (2014, May 4). Cord or Knot Magick. Retrieved from Goddesshasyourback.com website: https://goddesshasyourback.com/2014/05/04/cord-or-knot-magick

Onofrio, E. (2020, November 22). What are energy cords? – soul to soul. Retrieved from

Soultosoulsessions.com website:

https://soultosoulsessions.com/soul-sessions-blog/2020/11/22/what-are-energy-cords

Ourisman, J. (2020, December 2). What Is Cord Cutting? Three energy healers explain - nécessité. Retrieved from Necessite.co website:

https://necessite.co/2020/12/02/what-is-cord-cutting-three-energy-healers-explain

Willow. (2020, April 16). Knot magick. Retrieved from Whitewitchgrimoire.com website:

https://www.whitewitchgrimoire.com/knot-magick

Knot magic spells. (n.d.). Retrieved from Hoodoowitch.net website:

https://www.hoodoowitch.net/2020/01/18/knot-magic-spells

ladyoftheabyss. (2012, March 10). Cutting the cord spell. Retrieved from Witchesofthecraft.com website:
https://witchesofthecraft.com/2012/03/10/cutting-the-cord-spell

ladyoftheabyss. (2013, August 15). Knot magick spell to heal. Retrieved from

Witchesofthecraft.com website:
https://witchesofthecraft.com/2013/08/15/knot-magick-spell-to-heal

White Magick Protection Spell - Knot Magick - Protect yourself from negative energy. (n.d.).

Retrieved from Magicknotionsandpotions.com website:

http://www.magicknotionsandpotions.com/protection.php

Frank, R. H. (2016, April 13). Luck is a bigger contributor to success than people give it credit

for. Atlantic Monthly (Boston, Mass.: 1993). Retrieved from

Kai, V. A. P. by. (2020, October 23). Money / prosperity / job spell herbal mixture and knot spell. Retrieved from Colibritarot.com website: https://colibritarot.com/2020/10/23/money-prosperity-job-spell-herbal-mixture

Kaufman, S. B. (n.d.). The role of luck in life success is far greater than we realized. Retrieved

from Scientificamerican.com website: https://blogs.scientificamerican.com/beautiful-minds/the-role-of-luck-in-life-success-is-far-greater-than-we-realized

Knot Spell for Career Advancement, Job, Money, Prosperity, and Abundance. (2020). Available

from https://www.youtube.com/watch?v=cDdF1DKCjMI

Martisiute, L. (2017, November 20). Celebs who became famous by pure chance. Retrieved from Therichest.com website:

https://www.therichest.com/world-entertainment/15-celebs-who-became-famous-by-pure-chance

Printed in Dunstable, United Kingdom